LIVING LIFE ABUNDANTLY

Dear Nancy,

May the abundant
life of Jesus Christ
be yours
always!

In His Service,
Johnnette
John 10:10

Living Life *A*bundantly

Stories of People Who Encountered God

JOHNNETTE S. BENKOVIC

PUBLISHED BY ST. ANTHONY MESSENGER PRESS
CINCINNATI, OHIO

Scripture quotations, unless otherwise indicated, are taken from the Revised Standard Version of the Bible, New Testament, copyright 1945, Old Testament, copyright 1852, The Apocrypha, copyright 1957, The Catholic Edition of the New Testament, copyright 1965, The Catholic Edition of the Old Testament, incorporating the Apocrypha, copyright 1966 by Division of Christian Education of the National Council of the Churches of Christ in the United States of America. Used by permission. Scripture quotations marked NRSV are from the New Revised Standard Version of the Bible. Scripture quotations marked NAB are taken from the New American Bible. Excerpts from the English translation of the *Catechism of the Catholic Church* for use in the United States of America copyright 1994, United States Catholic Conference, Inc.—Libreria Editrice Vaticana. Used with permission.

Cover design: Von Glitschka

Library of Congress Cataloging-in-Publication Data

    Living life abundantly : stories of people who encountered God /
    [compiled by] Johnnette S. Benkovic.
       p. cm.
    ISBN 1-56955-231-2 (alk. paper)
    1. Christian life—Catholic authors. I. Benkovic, Johnnette S.
    BX2350.3 .L58 2002
    242—dc21

                                 2002004474

ISBN-13: 978-1-56955-231-5
ISBN-10: 1-56955-231-2

Published by Servant Books, an imprint of
St. Anthony Messenger Press
28 W. Liberty St.
Cincinnati, OH 45202
www.ServantBooks.org

Printed in the United States of America

Printed on acid-free paper

    11 9 8 7 6 5 4 3

DEDICATION

To my son, Simon,

whose virtues of

perseverance and fortitude

have inspired and

encouraged me.

May your life be filled

with Our Lord's abundant love.

And may you always be a

witness to the Faith.

CONTENTS

ACKNOWLEDGMENTS

*E*very book takes on a life of its own, and many people are responsible for helping to "birth" it. *Living Life Abundantly* is no exception. It has been my great blessing to have had the help, support, and advice of many individuals whose keen vision of what this book should be has helped to make it possible.

Thank you to Servant Publications, especially Bert Ghezzi, who suggested the project to me in the first place. Bert has been an inspiration to me since my early days of "reversion" back to the faith. At the time, he was editor of *New Covenant* Magazine, and through his editorial expertise became a teacher, guide, and witness to the Faith for me.

Thank you also to Heidi Hess Saxton, who collaborated with me on *Living Life Abundantly*. Her good advice and counsel, her helpful suggestions, and her diligence to the task were all invaluable to me.

A thank you, also, to my staff of Living His Life Abundantly ® International, Inc, who "picked up the slack" while I worked on *Living Life Abundantly;* and to my mother, Johnnette Simon, who read the stories and gave me her insights.

And this book could not have been completed without the gracious understanding and love of my husband, Anthony, whose patience and consideration are a witness to me. Your love is my greatest joy.

But, most importantly, I want to thank all of the men and women who have given me permission to include their stories in *Living Life Abundantly*. To Marietta Jaeger-Lane, Dr. Jay and Jana Carpenter, Keith Sutton, Bryan and Susan Thatcher, Deborah Russo, John Evans,

Cindy Speltz, Liz Kelly, Rev. David Kyle Foster, Dr. Paul and Jodi Hayes, Dan and Bobbi Vaughan, Maru Ahumada, Cathy Dailey, Maureen and Marty Mueller, Theresa Burke, Donna, Dr. Francisco and Marie Colón, I thank you. Each of you has inspired me in ways you will never know. May God bless you for your witness to the love of God and the abundant life that comes through His Son, Jesus Christ.

If there are any errors or omissions in *Living Life Abundantly*, they are completely my own.

Introduction

In whatever situations we happen to be, we can and we must aspire to the life of perfection.

St. Francis de Sales

*P*ope Paul VI said, *"Modern man listens more willingly to witnesses than to teachers, or if he listens to teachers he does so because they are witnesses."*

My own journey back to the Catholic faith began through the testimony of a friend. Her example of Christian fortitude and perseverance in the midst of a great trial convinced me that grace was real and God had a plan for each of us. She not only spoke to me about Jesus, she "witnessed" Him to me. Indeed, because of her, my life was changed forever.

Throughout the years, I have been blessed to interview hundreds of individuals who, like my friend, are witnesses to the Faith—not so much because of what they say, but rather, because of what they do. Their witnesses of Christian virtue in the midst of life's circumstances have been a source of inspiration and encouragement to me and to my listening and viewing audiences.

Living Life Abundantly is a collection of fifteen stories, each of which presents a "witness" to the faith. In these stories you will meet ordinary men and women made extraordinary by God's life active within them. They demonstrate what the abundant life in Jesus Christ is all about.

My prayer is that as you read their stories, you too will come to see that God desires for you to be a witness to the Faith as well, no matter your circumstances. May the stories of these men and women inspire you, instruct you, encourage you, and lead you to a deeper appreciation of God's abundant life at work within you. And may their witnesses give you courage to be a witness to the Faith each and every day. The salvation of many is depending on it.

Johnnette Simon Benkovic

January 24, 2002

Feast of St. Francis de Sales

PART ONE

Overcoming Through *Christ* Jesus

Stories of Victory

Now faith is the assurance of things hoped for, the conviction of things not seen.

HEBREWS 11:1

With these words, the writer of the epistle to the Hebrews reminds the faithful of their heritage. One after the other, he recounts the stories of men and women who persevered, often in times of unbearable tragedy, confident that they would one day be rewarded for remaining faithful to the truth. Even in the face of martyrdom, they did not falter: they knew something better was in store for them.

And so it is today. In the next few pages you will encounter the stories of men and women who did not give up on God, even when tragedy and loss seemed inevitable. And yet, theirs are also stories of hope. Rather than allow difficult circumstances to undermine their confidence in God, these people continued to trust in the One who holds their lives in His hands. As a result, their faith became strong having been tested in the crucible of travail.

As you read their stories, may you, too, be challenged to offer up whatever is weighing most heavily upon your heart, no matter how great or small the burden may seem to you now. By surrendering the circumstances of our lives to God, we leave ourselves open to receive all the blessings He has in store for us. This is the way to lasting victory in Christ.

ONE

I Forgave My Child's Killer

The Story of Marietta Jaeger-Lane

❦

Father, forgive them; for they know not what they do.

LUKE 23:34

I was a young mother when I first read Marietta's story in a Christian magazine. With three little children of my own, the account of her daughter's abduction and eventual murder affected me profoundly. Somehow she had been able to forgive the man who had brutally taken her little girl from her.

"How do you forgive someone like that?" I wondered. Little did I know that several years later, I would have the opportunity to ask Marietta that very question.

Her answer did not disappoint me. I found Marietta Jaeger-Lane to be a remarkable woman. Remarkable not because she lost a daughter to a heinous and violent crime, but rather because she was able to do what Jesus commands us to do, "Love your enemies and pray for those who persecute you" (Mt 5:44). In that devastating and horrible time in her life, she displayed heroic virtue. Here is her story. See if you agree.

It is every parent's worst nightmare: A child vanishes in the middle of the night, never to be seen or heard from again. For Marietta, the nightmare began more than twenty-five years ago, while her family was on a camping trip in the Missouri River Headwaters Park in

Montana. It was a long anticipated trip and the family had enjoyed the park immensely. After settling her five children into their tent on their last night in the park, Marietta crawled around to give each child a kiss goodnight. She remembers that seven-year-old Susie was in a corner, and had been the most difficult to reach because of the camping gear piled at the foot of her sleeping bag.

When I stretched over and around the pile, I could still hardly reach her, my lips barely skimming across her cheek. "Oh, no, Mama!" Susie exclaimed, and crawled out of her sleeping bag and over her sister to kneel right in front of me. She hugged me hugely and kissed me smack on the lips. "There ... that's the way it should be!" ... I treasure that memory immeasurably, because that was the last time I ever saw my little girl.

Later that night Marietta checked on the children and discovered that Susie was missing. A large hole in the back of her tent was the only indication of what had happened to her. The police force, FBI, and other agencies were called in to help with the search, but all of their efforts were in vain.

A week later, one of the deputies working the case received a telephone call from a man saying he had Susie and would exchange her for a ransom. The call was authentic but the details for the ransom were incomplete. So Marietta used the media to tell the caller she and her family were ready and willing to give him the ransom. He didn't phone back. Three months later, another call came. Brief. To the point. The same message. And then nothing. For one year there was no more word from him.

During that time, Marietta was overwhelmed with feelings of rage and hatred. Though she rarely expressed it verbally, she was seething on the inside.

I wanted to kill the man who took her, and most certainly could have—with my bare hands and a smile on my face—if only I had known who he was.

As time went on, however, Marietta realized that she had to find a way to work through these damaging emotions. She "wrestled with God" to find an answer. One day, the answer came. She needed to forgive her daughter's abductor. This was the only way she could reconcile her tragedy with her Catholic faith, and ultimately, it was the only way she could attain peace within herself.

Comfort in tribulation can be secured only on the sure ground of faith holding as true the words of Scripture and the teaching of the Catholic Church.

St. Thomas More

Marietta's approach was practical. Though her emotions didn't match her will, she took positive steps toward forgiveness. For example, she consciously reminded herself that no matter how she felt about the kidnapper, God loved him unconditionally. This man was a child of God even if his actions didn't show it. Therefore, he had dignity and worth.

Marietta also decided that she wouldn't allow anyone to speak to her negatively about the kidnapper, nor would she speak about him negatively. Such talk would only increase bitterness and resentment and make it more difficult to forgive. Instead, she decided to apply the Scripture mandate and pray for him. Marietta tried to imagine the circumstances in his life that could have led him to do such a terrible thing. He needed God's mercy, not her hatred. Authentically and sincerely, she desired good for him.

None of this was easy, she admitted. But she persevered in spite of the pain, the suffering, and the heartache. She attempted to channel her anger into positive outlets—conscious acts of forgiveness, staying informed about the case, trying to be available to her family members and their ongoing needs, keeping up with the duties of everyday life. In time, she began to see the fruit of her efforts. An enormous burden was lifting from her heart despite the uncertainty of Susie's fate. Finally, she could sleep through the night and feel rested in the morning.

Contact With the Abductor

Shortly before the first anniversary of Susie's disappearance, the press interviewed Marietta yet again. She told them she wanted to speak with the person who had taken her child. And, on the anniversary date of the abduction, she received a call.

"So, what do you want to talk to me about?" the voice taunted her. Instantly, Marietta knew who it was. It was the man who had taken Susie. She was shocked to hear from him, but she was more shocked by her reaction. Though his voice was ugly and smug, mercy for him, true concern, and a desire to help him flooded her heart.

Marietta's compassion registered in her voice. When she asked the caller how he was feeling, acknowledging to him that his actions must be a terrible burden, he broke down and wept. Her concern for him was the last thing he expected. The man let his guard down and stayed on the phone with Marietta for over an hour. And, through her gentle and caring conversation, he revealed enough details about himself and the crime that the FBI was able to identify and capture him.

Marietta had only one request for the FBI: to meet this young man before his arrest and tell him face-to-face what she had said to him over the telephone—that she forgave him, hoped that he would confess, and sincerely desired he received the help he needed. In this moment, Marietta saw the victory of her struggle. Indeed, God had given her the grace to forgive and she had used it.

About this difficult time in her life, Marietta says:

> I've heard people say that forgiveness is for wimps. Well, I say then that they must never have tried it. Forgiveness is hard work. It demands diligent self-discipline, constant corralling of our basest instincts, custody of the tongue, and a steadfast refusal not to get caught up in the mean-spiritedness of our times. It doesn't mean we forget, we condone, or we absolve of responsibility. It does mean that we let go of the hate, that we try to separate the loss and the cost from the recompense or punishment we deem is due.

Marietta learned that Susie had been killed just a week after her disappearance. The request for ransom and the phone calls had all been a ruse. When the young man was brought to trial, however, Marietta urged the prosecution not to seek the death penalty.

By this time ... I had come to understand that God's idea of justice was not punishment but restoration. Though I did not know if this very sick young man could ever be "restored," I could not deny him that possibility. Also, I felt that to execute him in Susie's name would be to violate and profane the goodness and beauty of her life. I believed I better honored her by insisting that all of life is sacred and worthy of preservation, even the life of the man who had taken hers.

Upon hearing that he was not going to be executed for the crime, Susie's murderer confessed to four other unsolved homicides in the same area. Four other families came to know the fate of their loved one.

An Advocate for God's Justice

Despite her family's tragedy, Marietta remains committed to forgiveness, and has remained an ardent opponent of the death penalty since Susie's death. She does not believe the death penalty serves as a deterrent, nor does she believe that it has any restorative effect for the victims' families:

Loved ones, wrenched from our lives by violent crime, deserve more beautiful, noble, and honorable memorials than premeditated, state-sanctioned killings. The death penalty only creates more victims and more grieving families. By becoming that which we deplore— people who kill people—we insult the sacred memory of all our precious victims.

Susie's murder has led Marietta to work with victims' families all over the world. She has been a source of consolation and encouragement to those who have lost a loved one by murder, in natural disasters, and through terrorist attacks. No matter the circumstance, in every case, she is an advocate of mercy and forgiveness. Marietta has been a founding board member of Murder Victims' Families for Reconciliation since 1992, and is the cofounder and board member of Journey of Hope: From Violence to Healing (www.journeyofhope.org). She is a strong and able witness of the gospel mandate, "Love your enemies, pray for your persecutors."

Entering Into Forgiveness

Extolling the spiritual benefits of forgiveness, St. John Vianney said, "The saints had no bitterness, no hatred. They forgave everything." While we know forgiveness is good for the soul, recent scientific studies are pointing to the physical and emotional benefits of forgiveness as well. How, then, do we enter the process?

Marietta's example shows the way: it begins with a decision to forgive followed by practical strategies. Psychologists have helped to identify the fundamental steps in the process:

Admit the anger. As long as anger remains below the surface, it exerts power over us that is difficult to control. Admitting its existence is the first way to loosen its hold on us.

Identify or name the emotions or hurt involved. Ask the questions, "What loss did I experience?" or "What negative effect have I experienced because of the offense?" Is it a loss of fidelity, a loss of security in a relationship, the negative effect of rejection, the loss of our good name, the loss of a loved one? The answers to these questions point the direction to healing.

Express the emotion or hurt. Write it out in a journal, talk with a friend, confessor, or spiritual director, talk to the person who injured you, but get it out.

Exercise understanding. Psychologists often call this step "reframing." Essentially, it is choosing to reappraise what happened by considering other factors that we may have ignored initially. It is often the most challenging step of the process because it represents a move away from our pain to explore the reasons for the offending party's behavior.

Forgive and cancel the debt. Ultimately, the moment arrives to make the decision to forgive. It does not mean the pain will automatically go away, nor does it mean there won't be moments of regret or sadness. It does mean that in those moments we will admit the hurt and renew our commitment to forgive in spite of it.

Marietta's example shows that even in the worst of circumstances, forgiveness is possible through the grace of God.

Portions of this story have been adapted from *Not in Our Name: Murder Victims' Families Speak Out Against the Death Penalty,* a publication of Murder Victims' Families for Reconciliation (1998). Used by permission of the authors, Rachel King and Barbara Hood.

TWO

A Life to Be Celebrated

The Story of Dr. Jay and Jana Carpenter

༄

For thou didst form my inward parts, thou didst knit me together
in my mother's womb.
I praise thee, for thou art fearful and wonderful.
Wonderful are thy works!
Thy eyes beheld my unformed substance; in thy book were written,
every one of them,
the days that were formed for me, when as yet there was none of
them.

PSALM 139:13-14, 16

I first met Jay and Jana Carpenter when I interviewed them for a radio program about their pro-life activities. These two medical professionals were making an impact in the Tampa Bay area of Florida through an organization they helped to found called Professionals for Life. I admired their knowledge, dedication, and sincerity. I also admired the fact that they were willing to endure the hardships that accompany a public pro-life stand in our contemporary culture. But, I grew to admire them even more when Jana's seventh pregnancy gave them an opportunity to practice what they preached. Their strength, courage, and love of life are examples for us all.

Q remember the day Jana told me she was pregnant with another child. We were having lunch together prior to taping another radio program on abortion legislation. It was during the Clinton administration, and many of the positive advances that had been made in previous years had been all but lost.

Though our conversation was serious and intense, Jana looked radiant. She was pleased about adding another Baby Carpenter to the family. She and her husband Jay had six other children, and all were anxiously awaiting the arrival of Number Seven. Neither of us could have known during that luncheon that Jana's and Jay's pro-life mettle was about to be tested through the crucible of this pregnancy.

Signs of Trouble

While they were attending the confirmations of their two oldest daughters, Jana's water broke at twenty weeks gestation. Jay is a medical doctor and Jana is a nurse. Expert knowledge like theirs can be a great blessing in the midst of such a medical emergency, but it also makes it impossible to dismiss the blunt realities of the situation.

Jana and Jay were both aware that premature breakage of the bag of waters does not portend good things. First, when the water breaks prematurely, there is a risk of infection that can endanger the lives of both mother and child. Second, the bag of waters serves as a protective shield for the baby, helping his lungs to develop and preventing the mother's uterus and bone structure from pushing too hard against the developing skeletal structure. Premature breakage puts this at risk. Finally, losing the bag of waters usually marks the onset of labor. Depending on the point of gestation, premature labor can be fatal for the baby.

After the Mass was over, the Carpenters immediately went to the hospital. It was too soon—way too soon—for the baby to be born. Though a child has a beating heart eighteen days after conception, and is fully formed at twelve weeks, his lungs are not viable until at least twenty-six weeks. Jana and Jay's baby needed a minimum of six more weeks in the womb. If that time could not be achieved, the baby's chances for survival would greatly diminish.

Complications

The Carpenters arrived at the hospital where all of their other children had been born, and were advised to go to another facility. The medical staff wanted them to be at a hospital with a state-of-the-art neo-natal unit. At the new hospital, Jana was given a drug called Terbutaline to arrest the contractions. All seemed well and she was discharged. But, the following day, another massive loss of water sent her back to the hospital. An ultrasound upon admission showed that though the baby was under stress, he was sucking his thumb and kicking. These were good signs. The doctors then turned their attention to Jana and ordered a series of tests for her. When Jay was comfortable that both Jana and the baby were stable, he went home to care for their other six children.

Early the next morning, the situation took a negative turn. The regular obstetrician, concerned for Jana's welfare, called in a specialist. His evaluation and intended action were stunning: "We need to evacuate your womb, now!" he announced to her.

Human life must be respected and protected absolutely from the moment of conception. From the first moment of his existence, a human being must be recognized as having the rights of a person—among which is the inviolable right of every innocent being to life.

Catechism of the Catholic Church, 2270

Jana was shocked. She knew her obstetrician was aware of her and Jay's pro-life views. And she knew that "evacuation of the womb" was a euphemism for abortion. She couldn't believe the specialist was serious; her response was clear and uncompromising. "You are offering to murder my child; that's not going to happen."

But the medical staff was unrelenting. They challenged Jana with all kinds of scenarios. Some of them cut her to the quick. "If you pass away, who is going to take care of your other six children?" they asked. "What will happen if you die?" Jana's professional acumen came to her aid: "We were gifted with medical knowledge and understanding; I knew that I was not suffering from infection, and that the pregnancy did not have to end in abortion." Jay concurred. Though he was frightened for Jana, he, too, knew abortion was not the answer.

The attending doctors and nurses were implacable. As determined as Jay and Jana were to save their baby, the medical staff was equally determined to insist on abortion. But the Carpenters continued to prevail. They were firm in their beliefs and fearless in their convictions and they shared their position adamantly with the hospital staff.

However, time was not on their side. Thus far, the Terbutaline had successfully stopped Jana's contractions. Now she needed another dose, but the bottle she had brought with her to the hospital was empty and the medical staff refused to give her more. Panicked, she called Jay to bring her a prescription, but both knew the distance would prevent him from reaching her in time.

Jana was beside herself. Why was the medical staff doing this to her? Why didn't they care about her baby? Couldn't they understand? She asked the nurses these questions over and over again. And finally, she received an answer. The doctors' orders stated, "No medication." "Since you won't have the abortion," a nurse explained, "they are withholding the medication. You will go into labor and deliver the child whether you like it or not."

Almost as soon as the words were spoken, Jana had a contraction. Frantically she called an obstetrician who had been involved in Professionals for Life when he had lived in the Tampa area. Though he now resided in another state, the doctor still had contacts in many of the Greater Bay hospitals.

Labor progressed, and Jana knew if there was not immediate intervention, she would deliver her child and her child would die. Desperate, she bowed her head and prayed, asking the Blessed Mother to intercede for her. From the depths of her being the Memorare flowed, speaking the intentions of her heart.

When she completed her prayer, the door opened. An unfamiliar nurse came in and handed Jana two Terbutaline pills. Jana took them, and the nurse left as suddenly as she had appeared. "I thought she was an angel," Jana recounted. "In my mind that woman ... will always be an angel." The "angel" had been sent by Jana's doctor friend, and she had arrived just in time.

The contractions ceased, and the Carpenters decided to leave the hospital. It was clear that the medical staff posed more of a threat to their baby than the onset of premature labor. Every time Jana moved or tried to walk, she expelled more fluid, so Jay picked her up and carried her out of the hospital in his arms.

Who Will Take the Case?

Jana totally and irrevocably submitted herself to the care of her husband and to God. Once home, she went to bed, hoping against hope that she could buy at least the six or seven weeks the baby needed for his lungs to grow and become viable. Silently, she prayed for even more.

Some time later, an unexpected letter came from the Carpenters' obstetrician. In it, he told them he was discharging Jana from his practice. He stated that he would not be involved in their "pro-life folly" to save their son. Jana and Jay were devastated.

They both knew that a cesarean section would be needed, and, although Jay is a doctor, obstetrics is not his specialty. Jana needed an obstetrician, but who would take their case at this difficult juncture? Through their pro-life work they knew Dr. John Brady. He shared their views and he agreed to take over Jana's and the baby's care.

The needs were two-fold: prevent infection and build up the water surrounding the baby. The first need was met by keeping Jana on antibiotics. They were administered to her regularly through intravenous procedures. The second need was met through the intake of fluids. If the leak in the bag of waters is slow enough, the baby's urination can replace the fluid that is being lost. To help increase the baby's urination, the mother needs to take in large amounts of fluid. So, Jana began to drink ten ounces of water every hour.

Although this technique is not widely used in the medical community, pro-life advocates, including Dr. Thomas Hilgers of the Pope Paul VI Institute in Omaha, Nebraska, have had success with it.

A Time of Love and Fellowship

Life for the Carpenter family changed dramatically. Though Jana was bedridden, family needs remained, and time and again, God provided— most often through the help of others. Jana recalls:

People came every night with food for the family. People who had nine or ten children would take care of their families, then cook another meal just for our family. People even drove the children to swimming lessons.

Jay and Jana were overwhelmed with the generosity and love of their friends. Their care and concern gave them the emotional support they needed. Their parish community also took good care of them. Jana continues:

Every day a lady would come from my church and give me Our Lord in the Holy Eucharist. On Sundays, a priest would come and say Mass. Having regular access to the sacraments gave me [the strength I needed] to get through this time.

Day by day, God was meeting the Carpenters' needs and, though daily life required some planning, it was a time of real peace and contentment. Jana remembers,

Miraculously, I was happy at that time in my life. I was never bored, and every day that the baby was OK was a gift to me. I home-schooled from bed, and the children finished the school year. You get a lot of grace from God to do what needs to be done.

Jay, too, recognized the grace of God at work in their lives. "I was fearful at first of the task we had undertaken. However, with God's grace we did what had to be done. People came and helped us, and it was never a burden. The fear left us, and we were able to proceed with peace of mind."

That peace of mind remained for the entire ninety-three days Jana remained in bed.

Grief and Grace

Jana and Jay were grateful for every day that the baby remained in the womb. Each day meant continued development and growth for their son. And, as medical professionals, the Carpenters knew Jana's womb was the best incubator for their baby. Though it was unlikely Jana would carry the baby to term, she was trying very hard to keep him in the safe haven of her uterus for as long as she could.

Jana and Jay were not naïve about the baby's difficulties, however. Ultrasound tests had already show that their son had severe deformities and would probably never walk. What other potential problems he might have would only be discovered once he was born. And that day came on July 23, 1995, at thirty-three weeks gestation.

A test the day before had shown that the baby's head was being compressed. Though Jana's fluid intake had increased the water around her son for all these weeks, it was no longer sufficient. And, on the morning of the twenty-third, Jana woke with the baby's first bowel movement all over the bed. The Carpenters knew this was not a good sign. She could not put off the cesarean section any longer.

Dr. Brady met the Carpenters at the hospital. A priest friend was there as well. With him he had the sacramental holy water for Baptism and the oils for Confirmation. "The room was full of spiritual people," Jana remembers. This brought her comfort as she was prepared for the surgery.

Named for the two doctors who acted so profoundly on his behalf, John Paul Carpenter was delivered on July 23, 1995, at 8:00 A.M. He weighed two pounds, two ounces. Shortly after his birth, the medical team discovered John Paul had a major chromosome deformity that was incompatible with life. This tiny baby, for whom his parents had fought so valiantly, was going to die. His parents and brothers and sisters would have only hours to show him the love of a lifetime.

Dr. Newport, the neonatologist, intubated tiny John Paul and left him in the loving care of Jay and Jana. Cradled in the arms of family members, he lived for the next twenty-two hours. In those brief moments, John Paul knew only love. He came to know the love of God through the sacraments he received, and he came to know the love of his family through the caresses and kisses he experienced. And, thus, John Paul Carpenter lived the message his parents had long proclaimed—from conception to death, every life is a life to be loved and cherished.

After John Paul died, Jay and Jana massaged his tiny body with blessed oil to prepare him for burial. Though they were grieving their baby, they felt the tender consolation of the presence of God.

Their Fight for Life: Was It Worth It?

There are those who can't understand the decision the Carpenters made. Why would they allow themselves to go through this ordeal? For Jay and Jana, it was simply a matter of love and conformity to Church teaching. "We knew that [the baby] had very tiny lungs, and that he was a sick little boy. But we were willing to trust God for a miracle. If he had not had the genetic deformities, it is likely Johnny would have done well. It's a great joy to us that he is in heaven and sees God face-to-face."

In a real way, the short but powerful life of this little boy reminds us that in the midst of our difficult moments, God's will is accomplished through those who obey Him. "We feel the gift of resurrection for that child," Jana says. "I know that through Baptism and Confirmation, both of which he received, he is now with God. Today, we have an intercessor in heaven for us; his name is John Paul Carpenter."

* * *

If you or someone you love is having fertility or pregnancy-related problems, or if you would just like more information about the Pope Paul VI Institute of Reproductive Services, contact:

Pope Paul VI Institute
6901 Mercy Road
Omaha, Nebraska 68106
(402)390-6600

THREE

A Miracle on the Road

The Story of Keith Sutton

❧

No evil shall befall you, no scourge come near your tent. For He will give his angels charge of you to guard you in all your ways.

PSALM 91:10-11

All of us need the protection of God as we go about our daily lives. How many times have we been spared great disasters? How many times have difficulties and trials lessened in severity because of God's mercy? How many times have we experienced the providence of God in seemingly hopeless situations?

Perhaps the exact number of God's timely interventions in our lives will remain unknown, but time and again we each have had brushes with our own mortality.

In this story, Keith Sutton experienced the providential mercy of God as he headed to work one day. That morning served as a reminder to him that day in and day out, in ordinary and not so ordinary ways, God reveals His love, His compassion, and His faithfulness to us.

Keith couldn't have known what the day held in store for him when he awoke early on May 19, 2000, to head into his office at Allegheny Power in Pittsburgh, Pennsylvania. He was meeting an early schedule to open the plant at 6:00 A.M. for a safety rodeo being held for the employees. His mind was filled with the event's details as well as the concerns he had for getting his own department's workload accomplished. It was going to be a long and hard day.

At 5:00 Keith walked out into the dark and gloomy morning. The light but insistent rain portended a major downpour; he hoped to get to the plant before the clouds let loose. He climbed into his wife's Grand Jeep Cherokee, choosing to take it instead of his own Honda Accord. His daughter needed to use the smaller vehicle to tend to some errands for her prom being held that night. Already, Keith could see her dressed in satin and lace, beautiful for her senior dance. A smile played across his lips as he climbed into the bright red vehicle and strapped himself with the seat belt.

As he pulled out of his driveway, Keith once again looked at the sky. With this drizzle he'd have to be particularly cautious on the Pennsylvania Turnpike, the road he drove to work. Even in good weather the turnpike could be hazardous. Construction seemed perennial on the old road, and its New Jersey barriers, narrow lanes, and narrow shoulders gave drivers few emergency options. In the rain the road could be treacherous.

Turning on the radio, he settled in to the ride. Mentally he ticked off all he needed to accomplish at work before the day ended. He hoped he would finish in time to see his daughter off to the prom.

Keith made the left on to the turnpike and went through the toll-booth. As he entered traffic, the sky opened up and the light drizzle became a torrential downpour. The road was slick with rain and built-up oil. Keith knew how dangerous that combination could be. He had seen horrible accidents occur in similar conditions on the old road. But the traffic around him was accelerating and he needed to pick up his speed to stay in the flow.

As he drove, Keith's fingers closed around the medal he was wearing. Beth, his wife, had had the papal medal blessed, and given it to him for his birthday two months before. She knew how much Keith loved and admired the Holy Father and thought this would be the perfect gift for him. And it was: Keith had not taken it off from the moment she had fastened it around his neck.

The Jeep was approaching Exit 7. Keith remembered that there was a slight grade in the approach that flattened just before the exit. As he came to it, he proceeded cautiously down the slight decline.

And then, the unpredictable happened! The Cherokee hit a wall of accumulated water on the straightaway. The road, slick with residual oil, offered no traction. The vehicle lurched forward, hydroplaned, and was sent into a dizzying spin. Keith struggled to maintain control, but his efforts were futile. The Jeep tipped and began to roll.

Again and again the Cherokee cartwheeled. Glass shattered. Metal crunched. Wheels ripped from their axles. The roof caved in. The back end of the Jeep was pushed forward till it hugged the front seat.

With each slam of impact, thoughts rushed through Keith's mind—fragmented thoughts, one interposing itself on to the other: Who would open the plant? What about the rodeo? Lindsay's prom, he would miss the prom. Beth, dear Beth! Bursts of white light flashed before his eyes. Headlights? Was he dying? Had he died already? Time seemed suspended in this whirl of thoughts, sounds, images, and emotions.

For well-disposed members of the faithful, the liturgy of the sacraments and sacramentals sanctifies almost every event of their lives with the divine grace which flows from the Paschal mystery of the Passion, Death, and Resurrection of Christ. From this source all sacraments and sacramentals draw their power. There is scarcely any proper use of material things which cannot be thus directed toward the sanctification of men and the praise of God.

Sacrosanctum concilium, 61

Finally, the vehicle came to a stop. It was driver's-side-down in the right-hand lane of the turnpike. Disoriented and confused, Keith struggled for a point of reference. He looked up and saw that the passenger window was blown out. Carefully he made his way through the debris of the car until he could hoist himself out of the window. Headlights glared, and Keith knew he was in the path of oncoming traffic. Afraid that no one would see him, he climbed back into the car and waited for help.

The Rescue

Cars pulled off the road onto the narrow shoulder. Within minutes an ambulance arrived at the scene. The paramedics put Keith on a stretcher, adjusted a brace around his neck, and sped him away. Again, his fingers clutched the papal medal around his neck, and he prayed for God's mercy.

At the hospital, tests and examinations showed no serious injuries. Not even a bone had been broken. The emergency-room doctor and the paramedics shook their heads in disbelief. By every indication, this accident should have cost Keith his life. But he had been spared. Why? What was it that protected him?

Keith believed he knew the answer. Once more his fingers gripped the papal medal around his neck. It was the blessing of this sacramental, given to him by his wife. In faith, he knew it had been instrumental in protecting him against the danger he had faced.

Keith was released from the hospital and, when Beth came to take him home, he smiled at her with eyes of love, more tender even than the love they had already known. In facing his mortality, Keith had come to a deeper appreciation of the gift of life, the gift of love, and the gift of faith. And, later that night, he smiled through tears as he watched his daughter go off to her senior prom.

FOUR

Rescued and Restored by God's Mercy

The Story of Bryan and Susan Thatcher

ᴪ

*If we say we have no sin, we deceive ourselves, and the truth is
not in us. If we confess our sins, He is faithful and just, and will
forgive our sins and cleanse us from unrighteousness.*

1 JOHN 1:8-9

*In preparation for this story I listened to the first radio interview I
did with Bryan Thatcher. And, once again, his story ministered to
my heart. Perhaps it is Bryan's humility, or his faith and trust, or the
simple fact that his experience of God's mercy has been so profound
that it radiates from him. No matter the reason, listening to him
talk of his conversion and God's ultimate action in his life becomes
a healing moment for all who hear. I hope Bryan's story will be a
source of hope for you.*

*B*ryan was a driven man. From the time he decided medicine
would be his profession, he worked at it with uncompromising
diligence. With a near-genius IQ, he trained in the best medical
schools, residency and fellowship programs, and quickly distinguished
himself among his colleagues. He was widely published, and his career
shined big and bright before him. He was headed for success.

And he was not disappointed. For years, Bryan was a prominent
physician with a lucrative practice. He seemed to have everything—a

lovely wife and family, a noteworthy career, social standing, professional status, and all the comforts of financial success. On the outside, everything looked good. What was happening on the inside, however, was quite another matter.

Emotionally and spiritually, Bryan was bankrupt. For all of his material and professional success, he was miserable. He was not at peace. He worked harder to fill the void growing within him, but the harder he worked, the worse he felt. What is more, his intense schedule was taking a toll on his marriage. He and his wife, Susan, were growing further and further apart. Communication had broken down between them, and this negatively affected every aspect of their marriage. Their life together as a couple was unraveling.

Soon, Bryan sought solaces, and initially he found it in the arms of other women. But rather than bringing him comfort, his infidelity only produced more distress. His misery became compounded by guilt and the shame of his sin. His life was a disaster. Brian recalls the intense agony of this time:

> I could only reach up and ask Our Lord, "Jesus, Son of David, have pity on me." I had hit such a bottom that I realized that I was nothing. I had everything materialistically, but it meant nothing. There was so much pain in my soul and in my heart. I had to just say, "Lord help me, help me, help me. Get me out of this."

Around that time a friend sent Bryan literature about the message of Divine Mercy. St. Faustina Kowalska was a Polish nun who lived in the first half of the twentieth century. Though poor and uneducated, the Lord chose her to communicate the message of His love. Her private revelation is preserved in her *Diary.*

In this diary, she writes that communion with God ought to be the center of our lives. Her *Diary* proclaims that God's love for us knows no limits. We need not live under a cloud of guilt, shame, or fear. If we acknowledge our sin, the Lord wipes it away. *"The greater the sinner, the greater the right to my mercy,"* Our Lord told St. Faustina (*Diary*, 723).

These words struck Bryan at the deepest level of his being. He knew God was calling him to the fount of His mercy. There, in the Sacred Heart of Jesus, he could find the peace he so desperately needed. For the first time in a long time, Bryan felt hope.

But he also knew his journey had to begin with honesty. He needed to take stock of where he was and what had gotten him there.

Once we start moving to the right or left of ... [the straight path,] then it's easier to go a little bit more, and a little bit more, and I would find myself on slippery slopes. I thought I could master the slippery slope, talking myself into anything, and finally after a period of time I was in a natural disaster....

[Finally, I had] to be totally honest with myself ... Why am I doing the things I am doing? I actually had to seek professional counseling. Now here's this person who has a near-genius I.Q., many years of training, and I couldn't figure it out myself. I didn't have the skills to handle the situation. And I had to turn to God and seek help.

Through God's grace and good counseling, Bryan began to discover the truth of his situation. Although he wanted to be freed from the misery he had created, he also wanted to be master of his own fate. He needed to be in control. He had to figure things out. He wanted to stay in charge. His training had taught him that, and it was hard to give it up.

He also discovered that he was attached to his accomplishments. His profession, his income, his possessions were very important to him, and he had placed these above his family and above his God.

Plato says the unexamined life is not worth living, and St. Teresa of Avila says that without self-knowledge there is no spiritual growth. For Bryan, this time of self-examination was a tough and lengthy process, but through it he saw he needed a complete change of heart, a real conversion, a turning back to God. And, he knew he could not do it on his own.

My mercy is greater than your sins and those of the entire world.... Come, then, with trust to draw from this fountain. I never reject a contrite heart.

Jesus to St. Faustina Kowalska from her *Diary*, 1485

Bryan took St. Faustina's words seriously and went to the Source of Mercy. He began to go to daily Mass and to regular confession, and he received the Eucharist frequently. He added prayer to his daily schedule, cut back on his professional commitments, and began to work on his marriage.

I needed to talk to my wife. I needed to work as hard on my marriage as I did at my job. Marriage is the first ministry. I had to refocus what was important in my life.

A Tested Trust

A dramatic change began to take place in Bryan. Susan noticed it, and in time their marriage was healed. Bryan knows it was grace from Jesus, the Divine Mercy, that enabled her to forgive him and allowed them to set their life on a new course.

The Thatchers continued to work on the areas of their marriage that had been damaged by the storms of the past. They spent family time together at a variety of spiritually beneficial activities, and made a family trip to Italy specifically to view the many Eucharistic miracles. They also started to host a number of Catholic functions. Eventually, the Thatchers began to feel called to a specific outreach an apostolate that would help others come to a deeper appreciation of the Divine Mercy and the great gift of the Eucharist.

Bryan and Susan also desired to have another child, one who would be the fruit of their new life together, but this desire proved difficult. In three years, they lost three children to miscarriages. For each, Bryan planted a rosebush in their backyard in remembrance. One baby they named Maria Faustina in gratitude to the saint who had given them so much.

Through God's grace, Susan conceived again, and this time she carried the baby to term. On September 9, 1995, following a long and difficult labor that nearly cost him his life, John Paul was born. He was a happy baby who radiated the peace and contentment Bryan and Susan were experiencing.

About a year after John Paul's birth, Bryan was working in the backyard of their home preparing for a Mass that was going to be held there that night. He opened the pool gate to go inside when he was called away to help his older son. Shortly thereafter, Bryan left his home to drive his daughters to swimming practice. He completely forgot the pool gate was open.

The cell phone rang as Bryan was making his way through traffic. Frantically, his ten-year-old son told him that John Paul was dead. The pool gate had been left open and the baby had fallen into the water and drowned. Susan had just returned home from caring for a neighbor's child and was trying to revive him. Bryan instructed his son to hang up and call 911.

On the drive home, I began praying with all my heart, asking Jesus to have mercy on John Paul and me. I was struck with tremendous guilt as I realized that I had left the pool gate open.

John Paul had been such a source of joy; he gave hope to many families that God's love can carry people through the greatest depths of sorrow. On the way home, as I was praying to Jesus, and invoking Our Lady and all the saints, I realized that at this moment I needed trust. I had been telling others about Divine Mercy and the need for trust for several years, and now the time had come for me to live what I had been telling others.

Bryan drove as fast as he could. It seemed he got every red light along the way. At one particularly busy intersection, he cried aloud to God. Remembering the story of Abraham offering Isaac on the altar, Bryan offered John Paul back to the Lord. "God, God, John Paul means so much to me. But if it's Your will to take him, I'm going to offer him back to You, like Abraham did with his son Isaac. I have to trust in You.

"God, John Paul has been so healing for us. A beautiful child. I give him back to You. Thank You for the time You have given him to us, but he is Yours. Jesus, I trust in You."

When Bryan arrived home, the paramedics were loading John Paul into the ambulance; the child was semi-comatose and unresponsive. Bryan called his sister's prayer group and asked them to pray for John Paul.

Initially, the outcome was doubtful. However, over the thirty-six hours that followed, the boy's mental clarity improved. And within two days, he was perfectly normal and released from the hospital.

Three weeks later, Bryan's sister told the family the rest of the story. Her prayer group had prayed for John Paul as requested. The following day one of the women in the group called Bryan's sister to say that as she prayed for John Paul that morning, she had a vision of Abraham offering Isaac up to God. In her vision, Jesus intervened and returned Isaac to Abraham. From it, she knew that John Paul would be all right. Jesus would return him to Bryan.

Bryan was deeply impacted by the drowning incident:

The episode gave me a deeper appreciation for the gift of life, and I better recognize the fragility of life and the fact that God does not promise us tomorrow. At the same time, I knew that I had placed my trust in God during that difficult time No matter what happened to John Paul, I had been able to put my trust in Him.

Today John Paul is a healthy, happy little boy. Assisted by his wife, Susan, Bryan is busy traveling, speaking, and writing on the mercy of God and the great gift of the Eucharist. He founded Eucharistic Apostles of Divine Mercy, a lay outreach ministry of the Congregation of Marians of the Immaculate Conception based in Stockbridge, Massachusetts. It was not easy for Bryan to leave his successful medical practice, or for his family to give up the comfortable lifestyle they had enjoyed, but Bryan and Susan are confident in their decision.

It was difficult to give up my license to practice medicine, but I felt a deeper calling. We had to change our lifestyle; we no longer had so much expendable income, and we lived on savings. My wife and I began to refocus our priorities, and realized that nothing else matters: The world needs to hear of God's great mercy. The conversions we are seeing worldwide through Divine Mercy are amazing.

Within our own family, the progress is slow—we take one step forward, and some days we take two or three steps back. But as we travel, we are finding that this message of mercy and the Eucharist is spreading like wildfire.

Bryan Thatcher will never forget his moment of epiphany. His story shows us that looking at the truth of our situation and admitting our sin can be a life-defining moment. Like Judas, we can run away and fall into despair, or like Peter, we can repent and experience the mercy of God. Peter's way is the best way. As Bryan demonstrates, God can do great things through us when we are open to His holy will.

* * *

The Eucharistic Apostles of Divine Mercy

The ministry of the Eucharistic Apostles of Divine Mercy encourages Christian families to gather in small groups to discuss the writings of St. Faustina Kowalska in connection with Scripture and the *Catechism of the Catholic Church*. Over time, the groups are encouraged to do works of mercy with a focus on the lonely, rejected, elderly, and the dying.

If you would like more information about the Eucharistic Apostles of Divine Mercy, contact Bryan Thatcher at

Eucharistic Apostles of Divine Mercy
123 N. Kings Ave.
Brandon, FL 33510
(813)681-3699

Dear Heavenly Father,

The gift of life is so precious. Thank You for giving it to me
today. Help me to show my gratitude by loving those
around me, by serving those in need, and by making
every moment of my day a reflection of You.
Give me faith-filled assurance that, even in the trials of life,
You are there, and Your grace is sufficient.
You will never forsake me nor leave me abandoned.
I pray this in Jesus' name. Amen.

PART TWO

Experiencing the Hand
of *G*od

Stories of Healing and Hope

And Jesus said to him, "What do you want me to do for you?" And the blind man said to him, "Master, let me receive my sight."

MARK 10:51

No one knows how long poor, blind Bartimaeus sat by the side of that road to Jericho. Most people just ignored him as they hurried past on their way into the city, the very walls of which testified to the miraculous power of God. Jericho was an important place in the story of the Israelites; it was there that in faith they had marched seven days and nights before the hand of God knocked down the walls and delivered them from their enemies.

Now it was a blind old man who needed the deliverance. A kindly stranger told him who was coming. "Jesus, Son of David, have mercy on me!" he cried out as he heard the passing footsteps.

Eager to get to the next village by nightfall, someone in Jesus' entourage hissed at the beggar. "Quiet! Do you really think someone as important as Jesus has time for the likes of you?"

The commotion caught the Lord's attention. "Call him over," Jesus said.

"Come on!" The same stranger who had told the old man of Jesus' approach now took the old man's arm. "He wants to see you. He has a kind face. This could be your chance."

And a new disciple had his eyes opened that day.

The physical limitations of our bodies can remind us of the impermanent nature of our existence. "Now I rejoice in my sufferings for your sake," the apostle Paul told the Colossians. "In my own flesh I complete what is lacking in Christ's afflictions for the sake of his body, that is, the church (Col 1:24)."

While God does in fact use a variety of means (including modern medicine) to restore physical health, He uses our trials and travails to prepare us for the life to come. Suffering carries a redemptive charism, both for ourselves and for those around us. Our pain is not pointless, our tribulations do not go unnoticed. Whether we receive physical healing in this life or perfect healing in the next, our hope is in the One who loves us best.

FIVE

Food for Life!

The Story of Deborah Russo

❧

For surely I know the plans I have for you, says the Lord, plans for your welfare and not for harm, to give you a future with hope.

JEREMIAH 29:11, NRSV

I first met Deborah Russo when she was a graduate student at the Florida Institute of Technology. She was working toward her doctorate in psychology and was particularly interested in eating disorders. At FIT she was part of a research team studying the causes, effects, and treatment of this devastating disorder.

I had traveled to Florida Tech to interview Deborah about her professional and personal insights on eating disorders. Deborah was in recovery from bulimia nervosa. She knew firsthand the emotional and psychological struggles associated with this disorder. But, she also knew the victory that comes when we join our efforts to the power of the Holy Spirit. Here is her inspiring story.

S itting with Deborah Russo in the Florida sunshine, I found it hard to believe she ever struggled with a potentially fatal disorder. She radiated health and a general sense of well-being. However, these were somewhat newly acquired characteristics. Throughout her adolescent and young adult years, Deborah battled an eating disorder known as bulimia nervosa. That sunny afternoon, she talked with me about her journey toward healing.

Like many people who have eating disorders, Deborah's struggle began to manifest itself early in adolescence, but the roots of it went further back into childhood. Deborah's household was one of crisis. Unpredictability, anger, and volatile arguments typified her daily experience. Much of this was caused by her father's addictions to alcohol and drugs. Early in life, insecurity and a feeling of low self-worth began to emerge within her.

The family's general dysfunction was coupled with a preoccupation over body image and weight. Family members would often make hurtful comments about themselves and to each other about size, shape, and appearance. As puberty began to change Deborah's body, she internalized the family's negative comments and preoccupation with body image, and started to loathe the changes happening to her.

"I was filled with self-hatred and critical dialogue about my body," Deborah relates, "and at age thirteen, I started dieting behaviors."

Factors That Contribute to Eating Disorders

A traumatic family situation, a predisposition to addictions, and disordered thinking about image and appearance made Deborah an ideal candidate for an eating disorder. However, the prevailing mind-set in our dominant culture about body shape contributed as well. We place a heavy emphasis on physical appearance, especially a *thin* physical appearance.

From supermodels to sitcom stars, from screen idols to music idols, from professional athletes to weekend fitness buffs, the desire for an in-shape, perfectly proportioned body has taken over the collective mind-set. Billboards scream it, television flaunts it, clothing styles demand it, and impressionable teens starve for it. Fad dieting, the use of diuretics, laxative abuse, and overexercise are often warning signs that signal the onset of an eating disorder.

Current statistics show that eating disorders are more typical among females (90 percent to 95 percent of all reported eating disorders come from this group), with the greatest focus on Caucasian women. But, men and other ethnic groups are affected as well. In these groups, however, eating disorders are often underreported due to stigma and a lack of appropriate prevention and assessment tools.

Eating disorders fall into several categories. They include anorexia nervosa, bulimia nervosa, and binge eating disorder. As was the case with Deborah, the eating disorder is often a mask for deeper emotional problems. According to Dr. Frank Webbe of the Florida Institute of Technology, between 30 percent and 70 percent of those suffering from eating disorders have a history of sexual abuse, 18 percent have threatened or attempted suicide, and many have a history of depression or a family history of alcoholism.

The Struggle for Control

For the eating disordered person, control over eating habits often signifies an attempt to bring order and stability to a life situation that seems out of control or unpredictable. But, as the illness progresses, control gives way to compulsion and deep-seated insecurity. The person with an eating disorder finds herself trapped in a never-ending, never-satisfied cycle of obsession, food control, shame, self-loathing, and emotional pain.

Such was the case with Deborah. As she entered adolescence, dieting became a way of life. She began to overexercise and started to abuse laxatives. When a classmate told her she could keep her weight down by throwing up after she had eaten, Deborah added purging to her list of "weight-loss" routines. Soon, her days became filled with binging, purging, self-loathing, insecurity, shame, and depression.

I went from restricting my food intake, to binging, to purging my food, to a tremendous sense of being out of control. What I thought would give me control created chaos and brought me to despair. I was very depressed.

The eating disorder robbed me of any self-esteem I might have had, and it brought on great shame and secrecy. I felt disconnected from myself and others, like I was nothing—weak, useless, so torn up that I felt as though I would have fallen over and died if someone would have blown on me.

Ironically, Deborah's cycle of restriction, binging, and purging never brought the weight loss she desired. Though her weight fluctuated, she never lost a significant number of pounds. This increased her frustration and her zeal for her "regimen."

By the time Deborah entered college, her eating disorder was out of control and her behavior was compulsive and alarming. She was eating until physically sick and purging three to five times a week. And, her forced vomiting was leading to serious complications. Her carotic glands were consistently swollen, she had broken blood vessels around her eyes and face, the enamel of her teeth was decaying, she suffered from cardiac arrhythmia, and had severe stomachaches caused by serious gastrointestinal problems. Her physical condition added fear to her depression, and she sank to a deeper level of despair. To escape the pain, she had begun to use drugs and alcohol. How would she make it out of this pit she had dug for herself?

A Glimmer of Hope

Though Deborah was raised Catholic, her faith had succumbed to her illness. She had no real relationship with God and doubted if He even existed. But one day her deteriorating condition brought her to her knees. Sick and suffering, a prayer rose from the depths of her soul.

In a moment of near despair following yet another purging episode, Deborah got on her knees and reached out for the One who is greater than every difficulty. She turned to the One who can give purpose to every suffering and bring good out of every evil. She sought the One who suffered for our sufferings and healed us by His stripes. She cried out, "If you are there, God, please help me!"

A short time later, God answered that prayer. Deborah's mother had visited her at her college apartment. Unbeknownst to Deborah, her mother went into the bathroom where Deborah purged. There she sprinkled the toilet area with holy water, asking God to deliver her daughter from her emotional pain and her eating disorder. Deborah believes that her mother's faith-filled activity was a conduit for God's grace to act in her life.

A few weeks later, Deborah experienced the effects of that prayer. In a moment filled with God's healing presence, she was flooded with mercy and love, light and understanding. She recalls:

I felt weak at the knees and I literally could not stand up. I began to feel warmth inside and all around me, as a glowing light seemed to brighten the room. I felt completely loved, understood, and accepted. Something within me was being healed. Every fiber of my being was filled with a peace I had never felt in all my life. Tears that had been frozen within me from the effects of my eating disorder streamed down my eyes. By the grace of God, a healing of all my interior pain had begun to take place.

Deborah's experience seemed to linger in an eternal moment. And then, deep within the recesses of her heart, she heard Jesus speak to her, not in a voice but more in an intuitive sense. She felt Him say, "Deborah, I know you in all the dark places within you, and I love you in each of these."

The effect of those words was immediate. Instantaneously, Deborah was freed from the compulsion to purge. From that moment forward this aspect of her eating disorder was completely removed. In that moment, too, she was also freed from alcohol and drug abuse. Deep within her, a desire for a relationship with God began to bloom. She wanted to learn more about this One who loved her in all the "dark places" of her being. And, she suddenly felt compelled to seek professional help. No longer was she too ashamed to share her deep pains and fears. Deborah began to realize there was light at the end of the tunnel, and that light was wholeness through Jesus Christ. Though her physical, spiritual, and emotional recovery would take time, she traveled a straight and narrow path to healing, hope, and health.

Entrust yourself entirely to God. He is a Father and most loving Father at that, who would rather let heaven and earth collapse than abandon anyone who trusted in Him.

St. Paul of the Cross

Therapy played a significant role in Deborah's life. Through it she began to allow others to get close to her and she was finally able to accept the fact that she was lovable. She also realized that she was not alone in her struggle with bulimia. Others had suffered with it and they were there to help her.

While on her recovery journey, she began to see that she could help others as well. A desire to counsel those with the same problem started to develop within her. In time, that desire would yield a doctorate in psychology and a career focused on counseling those with eating disorders. From the ashes of her sickness God raised up Deborah's vocation. Truly, He knew well the plan He had in mind for her.

A Family Restored

As healing came to Deborah she hoped her whole family could experience the freedom she had come to know. For that to happen, everything had to begin with her father. She had found forgiving him to be a difficult thing. So much pain and emotional trauma was connected to their relationship.

One night, however, she had a mental vision of her father during her time of prayer. "He was about thirteen years old and being introduced to drinking, not knowing that he would be prone to alcoholism. I felt such empathy for him at that moment, like I was there. He was alone, and he had also experienced trauma in his life."

This vision opened a place in my heart for my father. During a later visit home, when I saw my dad I was able to say, "Dad, I love you." He said to me, "How could you love such a bum?"

At that moment I realized my father's level of guilt and self-hatred. I said, "Because of God." Years later, I shared the vision I had with my dad, and he said what I had described was exactly what had happened.

In time, Deborah's whole family sought the counseling she longed for them to receive. "We all worked hard to negotiate, to journey from violence to collaboration, and learned a deeper understanding of each other. Alcohol, drugs, and violence no longer plague any of us. We are grateful for one another and the work we have done."

Deborah believes that God desires healing and peace for all of His children, no matter the circumstance. She and her family are living proof that any crisis can be overcome if we let the healing hand of God touch it and cooperate with His grace.

In addition to God, Deborah credits three women for helping her travel the road to wholeness. First, she credits her mother, whose inter-cessory prayers prepared Deborah's heart for her experience with the Lord.

Deborah also credits the therapist she saw during those crucial months following her prayer experience. This psychologist had inti-mate knowledge of the pain and heartache of suffering with an eating disorder. She herself had overcome bulimia nervosa. Her counsel and example fueled Deborah's hope and increased her motivation to reach for recovery. The therapist's example also inspired Deborah to consider a vocation in counseling others with an eating disorder.

Finally, Deborah credits the Blessed Mother. After her healing expe-rience she began to pray the Rosary. Some time later, an opportunity opened up for Deborah to go to an apparition site in Europe to ven-erate the Mother of Jesus. While there, she received many spiritual favors and these blessings bore fruit for years to come. They led her into a ten-year ministry to teens as part of the TEENS ENCOUN-TERING CHRIST program. Ultimately, Deborah believes Our Lady's intercession led her whole family into healing, recovery, and reconciliation. For Deborah, Mary is a powerful example of what can happen when we place all of our trust in God, because, through Him, all things are possible.

Does Someone You Love Have an Eating Disorder?

If several of these signs are present, this loved one may need professional help. (Editor's note: For the sake of clarity, the person below is referred to as "she" because so many women are affected by eating disorders. However, these symptoms may be present in men as well.)

- Is this person constantly dieting, counting calories, or exercising to exhaustion?
- Does she cut food into small bites, and eat only a few bites at any one time?
- Is this person defensive about her eating habits?
- Does she frequently withdraw from family meals?
- Does she go into the bathroom right after meals?
- Does she dress in a way that hides the shape of her body?
- Does food mysteriously "disappear" without a trace?
- Does this person frequently use laxatives, diet pills, or diuretics?
- Does this person complain about stomachaches?
- Is she getting a puffy "chipmunk" look to the face, have broken blood vessels around the eyes or face, or decaying tooth enamel?

If you have answered "Yes" to several of these questions, help is available. Visit

www.renfrewcenter.com

or

www.nationaleatingdisorders.org

Questionnaire composed by Anita Sinicrope Maier, Executive Director for the Pennsylvania Educational Network for Eating Disorders.

For videotape and audiocassette featuring Deborah Russo contact:

Living His Life Abundantly® International, Inc.
325 Scarlet Boulevard
Oldsmar, FL 34677-3019
(813)854-1518
or visit www.lhla.org

Six

Out of Darkness Into Light

The Story of John Evans

⮫⋇⮪

I will lead the blind on their journey; by paths unknown I will guide them. I will turn darkness into light before them, and make crooked ways straight.

ISAIAH 42:16, NAB

I remember vividly my interview with John. Quite frankly, I was amazed and edified by his candid testimony. It was clear from the expression on his face and the pain in his eyes that telling his story was not easy. But at the same time, he seemed liberated, set free, released by the experience.

I met John through an email letter. He wrote to suggest a program for The Abundant Life. *He asked if we could produce a segment on the sensitive issue of homosexuality. He explained how the contemporary arguments propagated by organized homosexual groups keep people imprisoned in a lifestyle that is severely disordered. He knew. He had lived it.*

There was something about John's letter that struck a chord within me. Perhaps it was the quiet courage it conveyed. Perhaps it was the common sense of it. Perhaps it was the Holy Spirit prompting me to move forward with John's request. I emailed him back and asked if he would be a guest. He agreed.

Now, here he sat in the studio, telling his story, relaying the painful events of his life one after the other. Listening to him, I sensed this was an anointed moment. Through John's story, God was reaching into the hearts of thousands of people giving them courage and hope, understanding and counsel, healing and restoration. And this is exactly what happened. The phone calls and mail we received from this program told us so. I share the story with you now, so that God may continue to touch hearts through this man's powerful testimony.

*C*hildren are meant to have good childhood memories: memories that give them a sense of security and love. Memories that provide them with a healthy outlook toward life, self, and others. Memories that help them grow from childhood to adulthood emotionally and spiritually. But, these were not John's childhood memories. Rather, John's memories were brutal and painful, searing with condemnation and ridicule. And, most often, these memories were etched by the one he should have been able to trust the most—his father.

As we sat in the studio that day, John recounted his childhood experiences. He told me that from the time he was a small boy, as early as age three, his father called him names. Terrible names. Hurtful names. Names that played in his mind again and again. Names that began to shape and form his self-concept. Names like "fag" and "queer."

When John missed a ball playing catch, he was a "fag" or a "queer." When he didn't measure up to his dad's expectations, he was a "fag" or a "queer." When his father had a bad day, John was a "fag" or a "queer." And, most especially, when his daddy had been drinking, he called John a "fag" or a "queer."

Though he wasn't a falling-down drunk, John's dad did drink—a lot. And when he drank, he was unpredictable. John and his siblings lived in constant fear, dreading the sound of the key in the lock, not knowing how their daddy would behave once he opened the door. And so, the children would run and hide, staying put until they could tell what kind of mood their dad was in.

It wasn't only verbal abuse that John experienced from his father, but physical abuse as well. He was punched, slapped, hit, and bruised. Once his dad, when he had been drinking, smashed a wrench across John's face, breaking his nose and sending him to the hospital. Ironically, John thought this behavior was normal and a common occurrence in all families. He was twenty before he knew differently. But, by then, the damage had been done.

In his youth, John isolated himself from his peer group, afraid to interact in sports and games, feeling the sting of his father's ridicule even before an attempt was made. He would sit on the sidelines, watching, waiting for the others to be done playing the game. "I beat myself up instead of my father. I avoided things so these things wouldn't happen. So I isolated myself from my friends in these areas."

And this isolation led to other things. At age five, John was sexually abused by the son of a family friend. So scarred was he by this event that he repressed it for many years. Then it happened again. In early adolescence, at a time so crucial to the formation of a healthy self-concept, John was molested by one of the adults who led his Boy Scout troop.

John blamed himself for the incident—he had willingly engaged in the act and, being thirteen, he should have known better. Never once did he consider the truth: In his search for male acceptance, he had been victimized by an older man who *did* know better. Instead, he thought his daddy was right. He was a "fag" and a "queer" after all.

This idea, planted so early in his fertile mind, began to bear a bitter fruit. By his midteens, John could no longer cope. Ridden by guilt, a poor self-concept, and convinced that he was a homosexual, he turned to drugs and alcohol to ease the pain.

However, at age twenty-one things seemed to change for John. He was surprised by a wonderful event that promised to make things right. He fell in love—with a woman. They had a whirlwind romance and were married within months. Two children later, John was happy and convinced that the past was over. But his bliss proved to be short-lived.

Financial pressures began to bear down. They were difficult and caused him to worry, but what troubled him the most was his son. He didn't know how to "father" him and he was afraid to show him love and affection. Interacting with his son seemed impossible, because above all, John was afraid that he would "rub off" on him. And, God knew, John didn't want that. And so, he did to his son what his father had done to him. He avoided him. Though no hurtful names escaped his lips and no physical abuse occurred, John distanced himself from his son. And this caused him pain.

A Turning Point

To medicate his pain, John drank. And he did drugs. And he began an affair with an older man. For three years these activities continued. But nothing brought him relief. Nothing brought him comfort. He was disgusted with himself and with his behavior. He was disgusted with his duplicity. He was disgusted with the pain he knew he was causing his wife. His spiritual life was nonexistent, and he was disgusted about that. Finally, at age twenty-seven, he was ready to end it all.

John told me about that moment. The pain. The frustration. The disgust. The self-loathing and despair. "Everything was going to ruin and I was at the point of suicide. I remember I was in the bathroom, and I looked into the mirror and I saw someone who was just the most horrible person and it was me looking back."

In that moment, at the point of suicide, he cried out to God for help. "If you are there you better do something because I can't do it!" And God answered his plea. The peace that surpasses understanding coursed through John's body, mind, and spirit. He experienced the invigorating power of the Holy Spirit setting him free, releasing him from the bondage of sin and the sting of reproach. He felt the love of the Father flow into his heart, healing the wounds and injuries he had carried for so many years. And, he was fortified with courage and zeal to set his life straight.

God does not command impossible things, but, in commanding, He admonishes us both to do what you can do, and to seek His grace to do what you cannot do.

St. Augustine

Immediately, John headed for the church. He broke off his sinful relationship. He sought the Sacrament of Reconciliation. He joined AA and became sober. He began to work on his family life. And he went into therapy. Through the constant love and support of his wife, through counseling, and through the unconditional love of God the Father, John's life was changed. He practiced the holy advice given by

St. Paul to the Ephesians, *"Put off your old nature which belongs to your former manner of life and is corrupt through deceitful lusts, and be renewed in the spirit of your minds, and put on the new nature, created after the likeness of God in true righteousness and holiness"* (Eph 4:22-24). At the crossroads of life and death, John chose life and he became a new man in Christ Jesus.

John's story has value for each of us. It reminds us that God desires to work in each of our lives and to set us free from all that holds us captive, from all that keeps us in bondage, from all that separates us from His love. Each and every day, God is looking for ways to show us that He can make all things new. What is He showing you today, right now, this minute? Will you, like John, say "yes" to the wholeness and hope God holds out for you? I pray so.

Courage

Father John Harvey, a priest with the Oblates of St. Francis de Sales, has been working with individuals struggling with sexual identity and chastity issues since 1980. Through the organization he founded called *Courage*, individuals have an opportunity to place their same sex attraction, as well as its attenuating difficulties, within the broader context of their Catholic faith. Support groups provide powerful assistance in helping members confront long-standing tendencies and habits, while at the same time offering solace and understanding.

The following set of goals defines the mission and purpose of *Courage*. These goals were developed by the initial *Courage* members:

- To live chaste lives in accordance with the Roman Catholic Church's teaching on homosexuality.

- To dedicate one's life to Christ through service to others, spiritual reading, prayer, meditation, spiritual direction, frequent attendance at Mass, and the frequent reception of the Sacraments of Penance and Holy Eucharist.

- To foster a spirit of fellowship in which all may share thoughts and experiences, and so ensure that no one will have to face the problems of homosexuality alone.

- To be mindful of the truth that chaste friendships are not only possible but necessary in a celibate Christian life, and in doing so to provide encouragement to one another in forming and sustaining them.

- To live lives that may serve as good examples to others.

For more information on *Courage*, contact the Courage central office at (212)268-1010 or visit

http://CourageRC.net

SEVEN

More Than a Conqueror
The Story of Cindy Speltz

~❦~

Who shall separate us from the love of Christ? Shall tribulation, or distress, or persecution, or famine, or nakedness, or peril, or sword?... No, in all these things we are more than conquerors through him who loved us.

ROMANS 8:35, 37

For the believer, the light of the Paschal Mystery imbues all of life's events. In its crucible, sorrows and sufferings are forged into fire-tried gold. Trials and tribulations radiate purpose and meaning. The shimmering light of God's presence infuses the ordinary and mundane. Cindy's story is a testimony to God's providence and mercy. From near death and utter desolation, Our Lord lifted her up, redeemed her trauma and trial, and gave it value and worth. Indeed, Cindy's life experience is a source of strength for all of us as we seek to live out the Paschal Mystery in our own lives. Let's meet Cindy.

S he had come to expect the unexpected, each day writing out a new story of uncertainty and confusion. One particular day in the kitchen, Daddy held a knife to his own throat, threatening to slit it wide open. Mommy stood behind him, applauding, as if to cheer him on. That day Cindy was really confused. And scared.

But today was different. Daddy's voice sounded hollow. Like the feeling in her stomach each time Mommy walked out the door dressed like a fairy princess. She didn't like those nights, except seeing Mommy look so pretty. Those nights Mommy didn't say good-bye and wouldn't look at her when she told her to watch the babies and make sure they didn't get into trouble. She would search Mommy's face, looking at her eyes, hoping for a contact that never did come.

Daddy's voice sounded hollow when he told his kids to put their clothes into paper bags. He was taking them to a place where there were a lot of other children.

Cindy did what he said. She didn't mind how hollow her Daddy sounded. Hollow was better than drunk. Bruise marks across her back and legs still stung from their most recent encounter with his strap. He would get terribly angry when he had been drinking, coming home all red in the face, screaming at her and telling her that she looked just like her mother. Then he'd take the strap, and the beating would begin.

Some beatings were worse than others, but she was getting pretty good at not crying. Somehow it felt good not to give in to the tears. It made Daddy really mad, though, and that was too bad. His face would get all the redder and the beatings would last all the longer. But, still, it felt good not to give in.

She picked up her paper bag of clothes, and helped the little ones with theirs. She wondered where they were going. Was Mommy going, too? How long would they stay?

At the Orphanage

Cindy remembered pulling up to the building in her daddy's car. It was a hot summer's day and the sun glowed like furnace heat off the sides of the big, imposing structure. A wrought iron fence surrounded the building and there was a big sign with words on it. She couldn't read it too well. The words were mighty long for a six-year-old. But they looked important and official, like the words on government buildings and the post office.

Daddy took her and her brothers and sisters into a big room that looked like a living room. A nun dressed all in white came into the room. No words. Eyes sealed the agreement in a silence that stretched to eternity. And then Daddy was gone.

Other nuns suddenly swooped down upon them like great white birds, dividing them up by gender and age. White wings flashing, flitting, fluttering, flying. It was all too fast. What was happening? Where had Daddy gone? Where was Mommy, and why hadn't she come? Questions, questions, questions. And no answers. Only silence and the touch of a great white wing on her back, gently guiding her down the corridor.

The Lady in the Garden

Though Cindy settled into the routine of the orphanage, the separation from her brothers and sisters weighed upon her relentlessly. Every Sunday at Mass she would strain to find them amid the flock of other orphans neatly arranged by gender and age. Little birds sitting obediently in their nests, close by the sisters in white. She drew comfort in just looking at them.

She worried for her brothers and sisters, but there was nothing she could do. Nothing, except visit the Lady in the garden. Every day at recess she visited the shrine of the Blessed Mother at the playground's edge. It was peaceful there and the flowers were pretty. How she longed to put a blossom into the statue's hand! She didn't, of course. Flower picking was forbidden. But she could give Our Lady her heart. And she did.

She told the Blessed Mother of the pain locked so tightly inside. Of her worry, her loneliness and sorrow. Of her heartache. In those gentle moments she felt the profound relief that only a mother's love can bring.

Visitors

Days turned into weeks, and the weeks quickly into years. Little from the outside ever made its way through that wrought iron fence and those big doors. And when it did, it always brought pain.

Like the two visits her mother had made. Each time Mommy had looked strange. Her eyes were large and vacant, either seeing something no one else could see, or seeing nothing at all. And she didn't even know her little girl. That hurt deeply, like a knife plunging into her heart. Not long after, she discovered where Daddy had taken Mommy the day he had brought them to the orphanage: a mental institution. It was there the fairy princess had lost her beauty and her mind.

More years passed. There were no more visits from Mommy or anyone else. Then one day a newspaper clipping was handed to her without explanation. "Mother of Seven Found Hanged in Basement." It took a moment for the woman's name to register. But it did. Mommy was gone. Really gone.

Cindy drew nearer still to the lovely woman in the garden. The one she could depend on and whose love she knew. Then one day the wrought iron gate opened again, and a visitor came to take her and her brothers and sisters home.

The judge had made a deal with Daddy. He could have custody of his children if he would take them out of the state. The judge didn't want to see Daddy again. They were moving north, far north.

Together Again

As if a day had not passed since their arrival at the orphanage eight years ago, Cindy assumed the role of mother. And, as if no time had lapsed, the brutal beatings and the abuse began again. It was worse now that she was a young woman. His words were uglier, his behavior more unpredictable, and the drunken rages more intense. The only respite was when he was gone. He left the children for weeks at a time. The toilets didn't work. The refrigerator was chained shut. Heat was rare. But these were the quiet moments. When he came home, who knew how bad things would get? Only one would face him, and she bore the brunt of it all.

No one came to help. Or to discover what went on in that dilapidated house on the edge of town. The children were taunted and teased at school. No one really cared.

"Just leave them be."

"Don't meddle."

"It's not my business."

One summer night when Daddy was away, Cindy saw eyes staring at her in the dark. A neighbor boy had stolen into the house and had hidden in her closet. He entered her bed and had his way with her. Shocked and stunned, she lay there gasping for breath. She prayed Daddy wouldn't find out.

Three months passed. Daddy had been gone for several days. He came home and found dishes in the sink. He took his belt off and went looking for her. He beat her and threw her into the street. She was pregnant. And now she was homeless as well.

At the Crossroads

Have an abortion, people said. It's legal now. But Cindy wouldn't hear of it. This was her baby. Why should it pay with its life for the actions of another? No. She would have this baby even if no one helped her. But what would she do? How would she raise this child? She could barely take care of herself. Her future loomed uncertain before her.

One night in her fourth month, she gazed out a window into the sky. In the stillness of the dark, she heard a voice, deep and infinite. A voice that broke the silence and lit up the night of her soul with the light of truth:

"This daughter is sacred and of God.
This child is destined for great good."

As the words penetrated her heart, the shackles of worry and grief fell from her. She *would* make it, and she would make it with this child.

Cindy gave birth to a beautiful daughter, with heaven's own blue for eyes. She gazed into them constantly with tenderness and love.

Hard Times

Seven years passed by. Hard years. In the midst of them, Cindy married a man much like her father. He beat her too—with his fists and his words. She had another child. This time it was a strong baby boy. But her husband's alcoholism drained the blessings she had been given. It was getting harder. His abuse was getting worse.

One day his temper spilled over to the children. In desperation Cindy wrote a note to God, asking Him to give her help and guidance. After all, it was His voice she had heard so many years ago. He had rescued her then, surely He would rescue her now. She finished the note and then went to the priest.

In sorrow and suffering, go straight to God with confidence, and you will be strengthened, enlightened, and instructed.

St. John of the Cross

Father was kind and concerned. Cindy trusted him. He put her in touch with counselors who helped her sort through the misery of her life. With hope, she began the long process of recovery. She discovered her marriage was invalid. In His mercy, God had given her a way out. She knew she must take it, for her sake and the sake of the children. She began the proceedings.

It was then that Cindy got sick and was hospitalized with toxic shock syndrome. Five days in intensive care, near death and fading in and out of consciousness. White wings fluttered over her. Around her ... about her ... whisking her away. Who was that near her bed? She knew that presence. ... She knew that voice. ... It was the Lady from the garden. She was there beside her, caring for her, making her feel better. What was she saying? Now she could hear....

"You shall not die.
I will be with you on your journey."

What journey? Where was she going? And then there was daylight. The night was over.

New Beginnings

Though Cindy was weak from her ordeal, they finally said she could go home. Home to the children. How she missed them! They were her life. In her enthusiasm to come home, she had not anticipated her weakened condition. The children clung to her and she to them. Softly, she whispered their names again and again, just so they knew she hadn't forgotten.

It had been a long day. She pulled herself up the steps to the bedroom, clinging to the banister. Would she never get there? Looking up, her eyes caught hold of the crucifix hanging at the top of the stairs. In utter despair Cindy cried out to the One who hung there, "See how alone I am! There's no one to love me." And He responded,

"I know how you feel,
For you have abandoned Me."

She knew it was true. In countless ways she had left Him. She had let life crowd out prayer time. She had let struggles override sacrifice. And yet, He had always been there for her. In her darkest moments,

He spoke. In the midst of anguish, He comforted.

Pulling the crucifix from the wall, she cradled it and cried. She wept for Him. She wept for her brothers and sisters. She wept for her children. She wept for her parents. And eventually, she wept for herself. Sleep came. She dreamed of a long, dark tunnel with a magnificent light at its end. The light pulsated with life, with hope, with love. A power other than herself guided her toward the light. Anticipation filled her. A voice spoke:

"See how much I love you, Cindy? See how much I care?
Do not despair, my child. Rejoice.
Know that I am loving you. No one can love you as I do."

Joy was infused in Cindy's heart. Abiding, infinite, never-failing joy. Joy fortified by daily Mass, the Eucharist, and the Sacrament of Reconciliation. Joy increased through prayer and the Rosary. Joy, the Holy Spirit's own fruit, alive within her. Joy, joy, joy.

The joy sustained her during the eighteen months of divorce and annulment proceedings, as she struggled to raise her two children, and as she worked to make ends meet. And joy sustains her still. A reservoir of joy that cannot run dry, for its source is the heart of God.

Some years later, Cindy made a novena to St. Thérèse of Lisieux, asking to meet a good man to be her husband and to father her children. On the Saint's feast day, she met him. On the same Saint's feast the following year they became engaged. And on the eve of the Saint's feast the year after that they were married. He adopted her children. She calls him, "My good husband" and he calls them, "My family."

If you were to ask her how she made it through the horror of her early years, she would smile and tell you, "It's the Mystery, the Paschal

Mystery. Baptism. Regeneration. Resurrection. It always comes after Good Friday, you know."

Can we make it through the struggles and trials of life? Can we withstand the onslaught? As Cindy would say,

On our own? Never.
But through God, we can do all things.

EIGHT

Healing's Song of Hope
The Story of Liz Kelly

❧

Sing to the Lord a new song of praise in the assembly of the faithful. Let Israel be glad in their maker, let the children of Zion rejoice in their king. Let them praise his name in the festive dance, let them sing praise to him with timbrel and harp. For the Lord loves his people, and he adorns the lowly with victory.

PSALM 149:1-4, NAB

At first glance, Liz Kelly has much going for her. She is a talented and beautiful vocalist whose poetic soul allows her to capture truth at its deepest level and share it with others. Her voice, like smoky velvet, has an earthy quality that goes straight to the heart.

Those who know her story, however, hear something else: the mournful sound of one who has known suffering, and yet has not been destroyed by it. It is the sound of one who has experienced the healing touch of God.

Liz shared her story of victory and hope with me, and has given me permission to share it with you. Her story reminds us that God desires to heal all of our life's hurts through His love and mercy. In Him, we can triumph.

*L*iz had just completed graduate school when she found herself in a messy time of transition. She'd finished her teaching position, and the band she had performed with for four years had recently dissolved. In addition, she was recovering from a mysterious and costly illness. Equilibrium problems, roaring noise in her ears, and intense nausea landed her in the hospital for a brief time. Her condition puzzled the doctors and mounting medical bills added to her concerns.

Circumstances were exacerbated by the fact that spiritually she was also searching for answers. She'd grown estranged from her Catholic upbringing through her college years and began attending Protestant churches. She had also explored a variety of other religious expressions. "I was a mess at that time, very unsure of myself and vulnerable. I felt completely ungrounded."

Her lack of confidence and her vulnerability would soon be used against her. Feeling isolated and uncertain, Liz accepted a dinner invitation from an acquaintance, a professional man from the community. After the evening was over, he walked her to her door. A sense of foreboding overcame her. She felt uneasy. The man had an ominous presence about him, and he had been drinking. She recounts:

> *He walked with me up to my house, and something prompted me very strongly, "Turn around and tell him to his face that you are not going to sleep with him." It was almost as if someone was grabbing me by the shoulders and shaking me, giving me this warning. But I was afraid of being rude, afraid he wouldn't like me, afraid of him getting upset with me. In hindsight, of course, I believe this was really a moment of divine intervention. I wish with all my might that I had trusted it.*

Instead, Liz ignored the prompting and the man followed her into the house and shut the door behind him. Intuition told her what was in store. Years later, she can still remember her panicked reaction to his advances.

I tried to push him away, told him no, but he had pinned me down so quickly. Afterwards, I was crying and he kept asking me, "Why are you crying? Why are you crying?" He didn't think that he had done anything wrong.

Liz was stunned by his response. Though she had limited dating experience, she knew that something horribly wrong had just taken place. She was confused, bleeding, and in terrible pain. All she wanted to do was curl up into a ball and disappear. Trembling, she walked her attacker to the door. Liz just wanted him OUT, OUT, OUT of her house. He, on the other hand, seemed completely unfazed by the event. "No, no, you don't have to show me out," he said to her. Later, he even called her for a date. "It was just insanity," Liz remembers.

Like many women who are sexually assaulted, Liz blamed herself for the attack and feared reporting it. She had been through so much already and all kinds of thoughts ran through her mind.

It was my house.... He was a professional person.... They won't believe me.... I should have fought harder. I truly believed that I had brought this unwanted attention on myself, even though that certainly wasn't true. Still, I assumed it must have been something I had done.

The Aftermath

In the days following the attack, Liz found herself unwilling to face it. She vacillated between denial and feeling like "damaged goods." Everything seemed to be crumbling around her.

She remembers making excuses for her appearance the day after the rape.

My best friend saw the bruises on my face the next day, and I tried to explain them away. I was so full of shame and shock, I couldn't quite face the truth of what had happened. I didn't have the vocabulary to deal with something like this.

I remember driving around the next day looking for a store that was open that might sell a pregnancy test. I didn't even realize that you had to wait a few days. I was just numb ... could barely think straight.

And, at that time, I couldn't get an AIDS test for a year. It was horrific waiting that time period out alone.

Liz locked that night and its awful secret deep within her. And, in time, she resorted to unhealthy coping strategies. She had always struggled with eating issues, and she plunged headlong into even more serious eating problems. Liz would starve, binge, and purge. At one point she took on an additional seventy pounds. She was demoralized and her self-perception was being destroyed in the process.

My sense of healthy, feminine sensuality was stripped away from me. My confidence was completely ripped apart. I felt soiled, dirty, and disgusting. And this translated into every area of my life, personally and professionally. I began having thoughts of suicide. The longer things went on without the rape being addressed, I grew less and less able to function. I was completely absorbed in my own pain, either oppressing it or allowing it to leak out inappropriately at inappropriate times, not understanding myself or my own behavior.

A Song from the Soul

It would take years for Liz to deal with the effects of the assault, and when she was ready, it came out in song. Her album, *Anima Christi*, became the catalyst for her healing. All of her pain, all of her suffering, all of the emotion she had locked away flowed from the depths of her being and permeated each note she sang. And, for many others, her music became a source of new life.

People—most often women—tell me that this album has helped them to grieve great losses; something at a deep level cries out to God for healing. Until then, I was in so much denial I don't think I really understood the full effect of what happened.

Gradually, the pieces of Liz's broken spirit began to be put back together again and much of it happened in the presence of Jesus. Like a healing balm, God's grace soothed her soul. Before the Blessed Sacrament, her tortured heart found solace and understanding. The Rosary to the Holy Wounds became a lifesaving devotion for her. Christ's wounds spoke to her woundedness, and from His wounds she began to draw strength and life. To this day it remains her favorite meditation.

When blood no longer flows from an open wound, to the indifferent eye it seems that healing is near. Nothing could be more wrong; the wound that no longer bleeds is one that will never heal.

Elisabeth Leseur

A Healing Presence

It was also before the Blessed Sacrament that Liz met someone who was able to direct her to the professional help she needed. But, it was still hard for her to talk about her assault experience.

I had let it fester for so long, it just got worse and worse. My therapist asked me to give an overview of what had happened, but I couldn't bring myself to call it "rape." He would say, "So, you didn't want to have sex with him and he forced you?"

"Well ... that's sort of what happened. The thing I really remember was he kept biting me like an animal."

Then, very gently, he brought it around to say, "You know, in this country you can go to prison for that. He raped you."

I remember feeling relieved and stunned and ashamed all at the same time. But there was huge relief in calling it what it was.

At his recommendation I went to a woman therapist. Both of them called it "rape," and for a long while, I bristled at that word.

I knew this man, it happened in my own house, I thought I had brought it on myself. It is awful to acknowledge the fact that you have been touched by something that evil. Terrible, but healing.

Several months into her counseling, Liz received a call from a friend. Her news was startling. Other women had filed sexual assault charges against the man who had attacked her. "He lost his practice and his mind, and he had been institutionalized. I couldn't believe it— it was confirmation that I had not been responsible for his choices."

With this news, the fog of doubt and confusion about that night suddenly lifted. Liz saw clearly. She had done nothing wrong. She did not bring the attack upon herself. Her assailant was a sick man. That was the truth, and the truth was healing. In it she found strength and through it she found the courage to confront her rapist personally.

Freed Indeed

Liz had just come home from a few weeks at a treatment facility and found a message waiting for her on her answering machine. To her horror, the message was from her attacker. Even though she had moved to another state, he had tracked her down. She didn't know what to do.

Immediately I called my therapist. "Do I call him back? What do I do?" I had never charged him with his crime.

"I think you should pray about calling him back and confronting him," her therapist told her. "Tell him what will happen if he calls back again."

Terrified at the thought of speaking with her attacker, Liz wrote out what she wanted to say beforehand. But she could not have prepared herself for his response. When she called him back, he astonished her by saying that he considered her a friend. He was calling her for a little sympathy in light of his current situation. Liz was shocked. "You mean you didn't do anything to these other women?" she asked. "Of course not," was his response. "I would never do anything to hurt another person!" Clearly, her assailant was out of touch with reality.

Liz resorted to her written page. As calmly as she could, she confronted him with the truth. "You bit me like an animal. You forced me to have sex with you. I kept saying no, but you raped me. And you say you wouldn't hurt a fly?" When she finished, the phone went dead on the other end. He had hung up on her.

But what freedom flooded her being! What liberation coursed through her spirit! The bondage was broken. The burden was lifted. Something had happened in the spiritual realm. The truth had indeed made her free (see John 8:32). Liz recalls the moment:

I felt like a little child, running around picking flowers and delighting in being alive. I felt so close to God. By being able to confront [my attacker], I had been restored to that place of innocence.

Liz was released from the chains of the past, and through the grace of God, she was able to move forward with her life. Though she knows that her healing process is likely to continue for a long time, she faces her future with hope and confidence, trusting that God will give her the grace to overcome. Now she is an accomplished vocalist and writer who uses her gifts and talents to praise the One who set her free. In fact, her life has become a song of praise.

Facts About Rape

The U. S. Department of Justice reports:

- One of every four rapes takes place in a public area or parking garage.
- Approximately 68 percent of rape victims know their assailant.
- 68 percent of rapes occur between the hours of 6 P.M. and 6 A.M.
- At least 45 percent of rapists were under the influence of alcohol or drugs.
- In 47 percent of rapes, the victims sustained injuries other than rape injuries.
- 75 percent of female rape victims require medical care after the attack.

(All statistics are taken from Violence Against Women, Bureau of Justice Statistics, U.S. Department of Justice, 1994.)

If You Fear You Are in Danger ...

Liz advises:

- Trust your instincts. It is better to be overly cautious than not cautious enough. We must not be overly fearful, but we must be attuned to what is going on around us.
- If you are assaulted, talk to somebody. Find someone you can trust. Talk to a professional—a priest, counselor, or other trustworthy person.
- Know that God loves you and wants to bring you to restoration. The spiritual disciplines of fasting, meditation, almsgiving, prayer, and Scripture study can be invaluable aids in the recovery process.

Heavenly Father:

Today I hold my hands out, ready for Your touch.
If You only say the word, I know the healing will come.
Whether the healing is physical, emotional, or spiritual;
whether that healing is for me or for someone I love,
today I confess that I trust You to restore that which
has been broken, in Your perfect time.
In Jesus' name, Amen.

PART THREE

Coming to the
*A*bundant Life

Stories of Conversion

Jesus answered her, "If you knew the gift of God, and who it is that is saying to you, 'Give me a drink,' you would have asked him, and he would have given you living water."

JOHN 4:10

*S*cripture tells us that there is great joy in heaven over every soul that repents and turns to God. No matter what the circumstances are that draw someone back to God and His Church, it is a cause of jubilant celebration.

Of the many stories in the Gospels, one of the most poignant is a story of conversion. In John 4, a tired and thirsty Jesus leans up against the village well. Noticing a young Samaritan woman who has just drawn a pail of cool, clear water, Jesus asks her if He might have a drink. Surprised that He has addressed her—Jews did not associate with Samaritans—she obliges.

In the conversation that follows, Jesus notices the woman's spiritual hunger. He challenges her to turn away from her sin and the empty ritualism of her culture's faith, and instead, to drink deeply of the "living water" He can give. Impressed by His ability to read her life and marveling at His love, the Samaritan woman cannot contain her joy. Running home, she tells everyone she meets about her experience. "Come and see someone who told me everything I ever did! Could this be the Messiah?"

In the pages that follow, you will encounter two couples and a charismatic Episcopal priest, all of whom had life-changing encounters with the living Christ. And yet, their stories also remind each of us that this initial experience is but the first step in a lifelong spiritual journey. In his letter to the Philippians (1:6), the apostle Paul exhorts the church, *"I am sure that he who began a good work in you will bring it to completion at the day of Jesus Christ."*

May these stories encourage you, too, to recognize the hand of God in your life, and to follow even more closely wherever He may lead you.

NINE

A Priest With a Past

The Story of David Kyle Foster

᠊᠊᠊᠊᠊᠊᠊᠊

*I have waited, waited for the Lord, and he stooped toward me
and heard my cry. He drew me out of the pit of destruction, out
of the mud of the swamp; He set my feet upon a crag; he made
firm my steps. And he put a new song into my mouth, a hymn
to our God. Many shall look on in awe and trust in the Lord.*

PSALM 40:2-4, NAB

*Occasionally we meet someone whose joyful and serene demeanor
speaks of deep transformation and profound healing. Such was the
case when I met David Foster. I had heard his story and read some
of his newsletters from Mastering Life Ministries, the organization
he had founded, and I knew that it could only be the Spirit of the
Living God who lit his face and shone in his eyes.*

*By looking at David, one could never tell that he had struggled
with homosexuality, or that he had spent almost ten years as a male
prostitute. His story is indeed a story of hope and healing, a testimony to the never-failing love of God, a story that proves no sin is
greater than God's mercy.*

When he was a lad, some would have looked at David's life and
thought it was charmed. At a young age he starred in a hit
motion picture. His blonde hair, blue eyes, and captivating smile
seemed made for the big screen. The son of a preacher, David's life

appeared as wholesome as apple pie.

But the picture was deceiving. His father was a cold man who often treated his four sons harshly. He was emotionally distant and sometimes overly severe in his discipline. Things at play were no better than things at home. Among the neighborhood children, David was known as a "goody two-shoes," a title that earned him the taunts and jibes of the area bully. Coupled with his father's severity, the peer rejection seemed almost too much to handle.

His self-esteem plummeting, David struggled for acceptance and sought ways to get it. One day he found an answer. Wild behavior and unpredictable antics could gain him notoriety. He recalls:

> *I cursed a blue streak, just to get laughs and to keep the neighborhood bully from beating me up every day. One day when the bully was in a particularly foul mood, I took off my clothes and ran around the playground, just to make him laugh. It worked. For the first time, I realized that I could get people to like me by taking off my clothes.*

David's solution was short-lived. Silly antics and stripping for laughs soon exacted a heavy toll. By the time he was nine years old, David was suicidal and sexually obsessive.

In spite of such interior pain and confusion, however, David did have a knowledge of God. During a Christmas church service when he was twelve, he experienced a profound sense of Christ's presence. As the soloist sang, "O Holy Night," David felt God's overwhelming love for him.

This sense of God's fatherly affection planted a seed in David's heart. He knew that he could find rest and unconditional love only in

God. Only in Him could he find true peace and joy. In time, this seed would lead David back to God. But not yet.

Divine Intervention

Shortly after this Christmas encounter, David left home. He soon found himself caught up in a double life, cycles of suicide attempts, and depravity. In the day he was an actor. At night, he was a male prostitute. For the next ten years, he averaged two to three partners a night. And one night, it nearly cost him his life. He describes this moment:

One night, as I was hustling on Sunset Boulevard in Hollywood, a very friendly man picked me up, drove down a dark street, parked the car, and proceeded to viciously strangle me with the clear intent of ending my life. By then I wanted to die anyway, and I stopped struggling so that he could finish me off.

As soon as I did that, God caused words to be spoken from my mouth—something that really can't be done while someone is pressing his thumbs into your neck so intensely that blood is running down your neck. The words said, "But I'm a good person." Instantly, the man stopped.

David knew Divine Providence had intervened in this horrible situation, but why would God spare his life? How could He even care about him? Look at what he did to earn money, what of that? David needed to know the answers. And so, he began to search for God in earnest.

At first David's attempts were fraught with false starts, but he kept pursuing, he kept persevering, he kept trying, and he kept getting up each time he fell. And, in time, David found the answer that resolved all his questions. He discovered that Jesus Christ loved him and had died for him; no sin he could commit could ever be greater than the mercy of God. From that moment on, David belonged to the Lord:

God had a plan and through one amazing incident after another, I ended up a month and a half later in seminary. Three years later, with the financial help of the man who founded Tropicana Orange Juice, I was awarded a Masters in Divinity.

By force of events, you made me chaste.... Chastity became a blessing and inner necessity to me. It was you who did that, O God—you alone. I, alas, had no part in it. How good you have been! From what sad and culpable relapses you miraculously preserved me!... The devil is too much the master of an unchaste soul to let truth enter it.... But you wanted to come into my soul, O good shepherd, and you yourself expelled your enemy from it.

Venerable Charles de Foucauld

A Path of Healing

David's relationship with Jesus Christ saved him from the pit of destruction. Through Him, David acquired the desire and the grace to work in earnest on the sexual addiction that had gripped his life. Not only did this work involve changing patterns of behavior, it also required ongoing emotional and spiritual healing. This work was not easy. Sometimes it was an uphill battle. But by cooperating with God's grace, David made sure and steady progress.

Early in his path to recovery, David was taught a great lesson by a minister whose help he sought: What we are powerless to do on our own, God can do through us, if we let Him act.

David recalls,

In the childlikeness of new faith, I believed, and overnight, God began living His righteousness in and through me.... He kept me from falling, He never let me be tempted beyond what He enabled me to withstand. He transformed my heart of rebellion into one of love and grace. And He healed, one by one, those areas of sin and weakness that led me into bondage in the first place.

The seed, planted in David's heart so long ago on a Christmas morning, was bearing abundant fruit. Imbued by the life of God, David experienced the healing love of Jesus Christ. And he knew he had to share this love with others.

Reaching Out Through Ministry

David's desire to help others led to the formation of *Mastering Life Ministries,* an organization which ministers to "sexually broken people." Since 1987, hundreds of men and women caught in the web of same-sex attraction and sexual addiction have received help, healing, and hope through this ministry's outreach.

Although *Mastering Life Ministries* is directed primarily at the bondages of sexual sin, the scriptural principles that are taught can be applied to overcoming all sins that exert a particularly strong hold on us. If you or someone you love is struggling to overcome an ongoing pattern of sin, these principles can lead to lasting peace and wholeness.

1. **See the temptation for what it is.** Temptation is not sin no matter how strong or for how long its enticement grips us. Even Jesus was tempted (see Mk 1:13). Temptation only becomes sin when we consent to it and give in.

2. **Recognize that Christ gives us the power to resist.** If we don't actively resist the temptation, we give it more power, until ultimately we act upon it. However, if we allow the life of Christ to flow through us, we can resist the powerful pull of sin. St. Paul calls this being "dead to sin" and "alive to Christ" (Rom 6:11-12).

3. **Reject the temptation and turn toward truth** (see Col 3:1-3). Turn your mind and heart away from the temptation and ignore it. As we read in Colossians, "Set your mind on things above. ... For you died, and your life is now hidden with Christ in God." God has given us powerful weapons against the enemy—weapons that have "divine power to demolish strongholds" (2 Cor 10:4). With God's help, we have the power to annihilate the enemy in every battle.

4. **Embrace new life in the Spirit.** "Live by the Spirit and you will certainly not gratify the desires of the flesh" (Gal 5:16, NAB). What does it mean to "live by the Spirit"? Pray; study Sacred Scripture; associate with good and holy friends; frequent the Sacraments of Reconciliation and Eucharist; practice acts of charity; seek virtue instead of vice. This is faith-filled living.

5. **Refuse to compromise** (see Eph 6:13). We must decide before temptation even presents itself that giving in is no longer an option.

The enemy is cunning. He seeks to trip us up where and when we are weakest. He accomplishes this in three ways:

- *Catching us unawares.* Sometimes a temptation will come upon us suddenly and with blinding force. To battle this kind of temptation, we must be ruthless and aggressive. Calling on the name of Jesus, quoting Scripture, and walking away from the temptation are all ways to overcome the lure of sin.
- *Getting us to compromise in small ways.* A road is built one brick at a time. And this is also how sin paves the road to perdition. Giving in to small temptations, especially in areas where we know we are weak, causes us to lose ground. Refusing to give in, even in little ways, protects us from giving in when larger temptations face us.
- *Convincing us that we can never overcome our sin.* Left on our own, this is true. But through Christ, all things are possible. Should we fall, it is important to repent, turn back to God, and get up again. This is the way of the saints.

6. **Guard your heart carefully by avoiding situations that might tempt us to sin.** Not all temptation comes from Satan. We often open ourselves up to it by flirting with our own weaknesses. We must ask God to give us a sensitive conscience, to reveal to us how we cooperate with our weaknesses, and to show us the habitual sin to which we cling. Ask and keep asking. The answer to such a prayer is a lifelong process of healing and conversion.

7. **Love God above all.** God has something better than the sinful baubles Satan offers. God has something infinitely better. He gives Himself to us. We get the unmatched privilege, honor, and comfort of His unending, unfailing, unconditional love. Reminding ourselves of this truth each time we are tempted will help motivate us to give a resounding "No" to the cheap thrill that Satan offers.

8. **Be both a lion and a lamb.** In relation to His heavenly Father, Jesus was a lamb, the holy Lamb of God. He did only what His Father told Him. He was obedient. However, in response to evil, Jesus was the Lion of Judah. He was assertive. He exercised dominion, authority, and power. Jesus was docile before His Father but combative toward evil. If we are to be like Jesus, we need to be the same.

9. **Let God operate.** Satan takes advantage of brokenness. He lies to us. He tells us that God doesn't care, that we are unlovable, that our sin is too great to be forgiven, that we are defective. Satan plants fear in our heart. He tells us we can never trust again, that intimacy is a sure path to pain, that God must not intend for us to be happy. Jesus wants to change all that. He wants us to know His love, His peace, His joy. God does work miracles. And He can work a miracle for each of us. He desires to set us free.

Mastering Life Ministries
P.O. Box 351149 • Jacksonville, FL 32235-1149
(904)220-7474

For videotapes and audiotapes featuring Rev. David Kyle Foster contact:

Living His Life Abundantly® International, Inc.
325 Scarlet Boulevard • Oldsmar, FL 34677-3019
(813)854-1518 • or visit www.lhla.org

Principles have been adapted from an article by David Kyle Foster. Copyright 1996, 1997 by *Mastering Life Ministries.* Used by permission of the author.

TEN

Beyond the New Age

The Story of Dr. Paul and Jodi Hayes

❧

I came that they may have life, and have it abundantly.

JOHN 10:10

In the life of faith, conversion means "turning toward God" and "turning away from that which separates us from Him." It means turning from unbelief to faith, turning from heresy to truth, turning from sinful practices to growth in holiness, turning from selfishness to charity. Such was the experience of Paul Hayes. His conversion back to the Catholic faith prompted him to look at himself, his medical practice, and his marriage. For him, conversion became the radical process it is meant to be. Here is his story.

*O*n January of 1994, I received a letter at the ministry of Living His Life Abundantly®. From its opening lines, I knew that a work of the Holy Spirit had been unfolding in the heart of the one who sent it. The letter began, *"I feel I must write this letter to you as a thank you for the ministry you are performing for Our Lord. I was dead to Christ just a few short months ago, and thanks to Our Lord Jesus' Blessed Mother, with the aid of many people such as yourself, I now have a life that I am converting to Him, daily."*

From that first sentence to the last, the letter revealed a man whose conversion was marked by a great thirst for knowledge and truth. In fact, it became clear that thirst for knowledge and truth had been the defining feature of his life experience. Until recently, however, he had unwittingly attempted to satisfy his thirst with erroneous concepts and false spiritualities.

Paul Hayes was baptized Roman Catholic and, as a young boy, he experienced an "intense desire" to become a priest. However, his father was an affluent physician and, as the family's financial security grew, his parents' church attendance diminished. By the time Paul was a preteen, the family's participation in Catholicism ceased altogether. This significantly impacted Paul. Not only did it interrupt his spiritual development, but it also sent him searching into various philosophies and ideologies for wisdom and truth.

Paul's teenage years were marked by the cultural climate of the 1970s. The sixties had bludgeoned the Judeo-Christian ethic with a hedonistic relativism and a neo-gnosticism that sought to eradicate moral absolutes and deny the need for a Savior. In these philosophies man held sway over his own universe. He could create his own morality and his own reality, and, through various methods and practices, he could purportedly discover his own divinity.

These thoughts and ideas attracted Paul. He was especially fascinated with Hinduism and Buddhism, and the many New Age ideas that were flooding the intellectual landscape at that time. As he delved into these religions and philosophies, the teachings of his Catholic faith receded far into the background. Soon, they became a distant memory.

Paul remembers this as a particularly difficult and confusing time in his life. In his letter, he wrote, *"I was lost. The only positive aspect of this time was having previously met, in the sixth grade, the girl I would later marry. We have been together since age eleven and the terrifying world of adolescent development was made a little less scary by her presence in my life."*

Turning Toward TM

At about age sixteen, Paul became involved with the practice of transcendental meditation (TM). He found it far more alluring than the hippie scene, and he and his girlfriend, Jodi, immersed themselves completely in TM and its teachings. Paul read book after book, and attended all the lectures and advanced courses he could find. By his own description, he was a "TM zealot" and the TM "cult" was to be his way of life for the next two decades.

Paul and Jodi were married at nineteen and they started their family right away. The children's births came quickly and seemed to keep stride with Paul's years of medical training. Their first son was born in Paul's undergraduate years; a second son arrived in his third year of medical school; and their third son came a few years later during Paul's second year of residency in obstetrics and gynecology.

All during this time, Paul was a devoted follower of Maharishi Mahesh Yogi, the founder of TM. He wrote in his letter,

Practicing TM completely leaves a person seeing this man [Maharishi Mahesh Yogi] as a prophet, if not God-incarnate, no matter how strongly people in the TM cult try to deny this. I converted many a person to TM, though few practiced it with the zealousness I did. I participated in all of the most advanced courses possible, even the ones dealing with "supernatural powers," as well as becoming a trained Maharishi Ayurveda physician. I was even filmed for a promotional tape of Maharishi Ayurvedic medicine. All three of my children were "initiated" into TM, and I demanded regular meditation from them.

With his TM beliefs intact, Paul completed his OB/GYN training in 1988, and headed back home to Kansas City, Missouri, to accept a position in a medical practice there. This position was not to last. Paul wrote, *"Despite all of my confusion about nearly everything else, I have always been anti-abortion, having had the good fortune of experiencing the witness of a strong Christian in my training.... Our repeated, long, often heated discussions culminated in my eschewing abortion...."*

When Paul assumed his new medical position in Kansas City, he discovered the physician he would be in practice with was an abortionist. The relationship dissolved and Paul and his family headed back to St. Petersburg, Florida, where he had completed his residency.

Within a year, Paul opened his own practice. He became known in the community as an avid New Age physician, and attracted patients from many cults and fringe religions. However, he remained openly outspoken against abortion and his statements on the issue led many Bible Christians to seek him out as well. In time, his anti-abortion views impacted more than just the demographics of his patients—they impacted his political philosophy, too.

By 1992, Paul described himself as "politically conservative." He recalls that the presidential election that year had him "keeping a close watch on all things political." This close watch led him to a discovery about the TM movement's new political party, ironically called the Natural Law Party. As he read the party's platform, he discovered that it was proabortion. This disclosure rocked Paul's faith in TM. He wrote:

There it was in black and white, a position on the sanctity of life by a group that promotes God-consciousness, allowing a woman the right to kill her unborn child. The carefully worded statement left the decision of the abortion "up to the person most affected by the decision."

My fourteen-year-old son said, "That's the baby, isn't it, Dad?"
The New Age movement, along with TM, was rapidly crumbling
at its cornerstone of sand.

Paul was profoundly disillusioned, and this disillusionment would soon become his doorway to conversion.

Coming Home

Twenty-five years had passed since Paul had practiced his Catholic faith. However, during that time one devotion had never waned. Throughout all those years, he had maintained a special place in his heart for the Blessed Virgin Mary. Along with a Bible and a picture of Our Lord's Agony in the Garden, Paul always kept a green scapular and a picture of Mary's Immaculate Heart on his bedside table.

One day in late spring, 1993, a billboard grabbed Paul's attention. It featured a picture of Our Lady Queen of Peace. "Why was the Blessed Mother on a billboard?" he wondered. "And what about this title of 'Queen of Peace'?" He was determined to find out.

Some weeks later, Paul learned that the Blessed Virgin Mary was reportedly appearing to teenagers in a tiny remote village in Croatia. She was giving the teenagers messages about the importance of prayer, conversion, fasting, repentance, and forgiveness. Paul began to read everything he could find on these reported apparitions, as well as on the many already approved apparitions of the Blessed Virgin Mary. He was "consumed to know everything about Our Lady and her message."

About this same time, Paul was flipping through the TV channels one evening when he stopped to watch a television program dealing with the New Age movement. In his letter to me, he wrote:

> *Of course, this was your show, and while I initially discarded most*
> *everything that was said, something began to gnaw at me. It was the*
> *truth that was so boldly being spoken on your show. You were openly*
> *declaring the deception of the New Age movement that I knew*
> *secretly, but would never speak. This is what finally led me to a point*
> *where I was able to proclaim that what I had participated in for*
> *over twenty years of my life, was indeed a cult and a satanic lie.*
> *What a breath of fresh air!... It truly is the experience of being*
> *raised from the dead. Your show allowed me to fully shine the light*
> *of Christ on TM, and destroy its influence on me and on my fam-*
> *ily's life.*

What followed for Paul and his family can only be described as the work of the Holy Spirit. Grace flowed in abundance and conversion started to happen at every level. His faith, his family, his practice, and his marriage would all experience a new beginning.

Paul broke with transcendental meditation and began to practice authentic Christian meditation and prayer. He frequented daily Mass and longed to receive the sacraments again. Jodi started to study and learn about the Catholic faith, and in a short time, they had their marriage blessed in the Church. On Sundays the whole Hayes family attended Mass and in the evenings they prayed the rosary together.

Paul believes that the Blessed Virgin Mary was a significant intercessor for him and his family during this time, and on the feast of Our Lady of the Rosary, the Blessed Mother seemed to prove him right. This day a very special grace came to the Hayes family.

Paul had a patient who wanted to place her child for adoption following the baby's birth. He and Jodi decided they would adopt the child themselves. On October 7 Paul delivered their baby girl. They named her Mary Elizabeth, and the very next month all four Hayes children were baptized in the Faith. At the Easter vigil just a few short months later, Jodi and the older children were received into the Church and Paul received the Sacrament of Confirmation. With Our Lady's intercession, conversion was happening rapidly for the Hayes.

Before conversion, it was behavior which to a large extent determined belief; after conversion, it is belief which determines the behavior.

Archbishop Fulton J. Sheen

Changes were taking place at another level, too. On the Friday before their marriage was to be blessed and Paul was to return to the sacraments, Jodi learned that contraception and sterilization stand in opposition to a Catholic understanding of the human person and the marital covenant. That evening when he came home, Jodi shared this information with Paul, wondering what he would say. Paul's answer was certain to have long-term effects.

Like most OB/GYN doctors, Paul prescribed contraceptives and performed tubal sterilizations. And, like most OB/GYN practices, these procedures accounted for about 70 percent of all revenue. Now, with Jodi's information, Paul realized that many of the procedures and practices he engaged in as an obstetrician/gynecologist were against the teachings of the Church. How could he reconcile this part of his practice with his faith? What would he do?

The decision proved to be an easy, albeit a costly, one. Paul wanted his practice in conformity with Catholic teaching. It, too, needed a conversion of sorts. The following Monday he sent letters to all of his patients saying he would no longer perform tubal ligations or prescribe contraceptives. He did offer them an alternative, however. He would teach them natural family planning.

Though his decision impacted significantly on the "bottom line," Paul knew he had made the right choice. And, some months later, he would accept a fellowship to the Pope Paul VI Institute in Omaha, Nebraska, to learn how to practice obstetrics and gynecology in accordance with Catholic moral teaching.

Marital Healing

As dramatic as these changes were, there was yet another area of the Hayes family that would be deeply affected by the conversion process—the marital relationship between Paul and Jodi. They shared this part of their conversion story with me in a television program we produced called, "Can I Right This Wrong?"

After Jodi had given birth to her third child, she began to develop medical problems that required surgery to her reproductive organs. The gynecologist suggested to her that since they would be working on that area of her body anyway perhaps she should have a tubal ligation. After all, the doctor told her, she and Paul already had three children. Paul agreed and thought the tubal was a good idea. Jodi signed the papers and the sterilization was performed.

The effect was devastating. Almost immediately, Jodi regretted her decision. She was plagued by a haunting emptiness that seemed to cling to her day and night. Areas of their marriage that were already problematic became exacerbated after the sterilization. And communication between them all but ended. They were into rough waters. Jodi recalls her emotions during this time:

I started feeling terrible about myself. I was depressed. I gained weight. I just couldn't really put it all together, but again, there was that emptiness.... I mean, you have taken away a grace that God has given you and you've closed that womb, and as a woman, you really have taken something away. And I could not figure it out. I was lying to [Paul], I was hiding things from him, the whole relationship ... I mean there was no communication. I literally fell apart. I didn't have a husband. I didn't feel like I was a good mother. And, again, [I] didn't know why, but I knew there was something wrong.

Paul was dealing with his own emotional reaction to their decision. He recalled:

I began to treat [Jodi] as an object.... not feeling any sense of connection or love, tenderness. I became very harsh with her, very angry, very volatile.... What she was doing was hurting me, and of course, what I was doing was hurting her. And there was this noncommunication that was established a long time ago that probably the tubal ligation didn't create but certainly finally severed.

At the time of the sterilization, Paul and Jodi were still very involved in the New Age movement, and Paul's practice included contraceptives and tubal ligations. However, following their experience, he began to do things differently:

The one thing I began talking with women about, even though I was continuing to do tubal ligations, was the regret factor. I found the regret factor very high in women, and of course, I knew the regret factor in our own lives.

Paul and Jodi continued to struggle in this area of their marriage even after their entrance into the Catholic Church. In an effort to find peace, Jodi regularly confessed her sterilization in the Sacrament of Reconciliation. One day, a confessor suggested to her that perhaps she should consider a tubal reversal. This suggestion seemed like a light in the darkness for Jodi. In it she saw a means of reparation for her sin and a resolution for her guilt.

Jodi shared the priest's suggestion with Paul and they agreed the reversal was something they should do. She had the operation and through it she experienced a profound change. The clinging emptiness she had felt for so many years was gone. It had been replaced with an abiding peace—the kind of peace that only comes from righting a wrong. For Jodi, the tubal reversal was part of her spiritual journey. "The reason I did it ... was to open my life to God," she told me.

At the time of the television program, Paul and Jodi admitted they were still discovering some of the deeper issues associated with the tubal ligation and their life together. Their healing process was not over. However, for them, the tubal reversal was a "tremendous gift" that had helped to bring them closer together. They were working each day to allow the grace of conversion to bring them the rest of the way, and they were confident that in time it would.

The Grace of Conversion

Like Paul and Jodi, all of us have areas of our lives that need to experience the grace of conversion. God wants us to receive that grace. He wants to make dramatic changes in us so that we might know the full measure of His love. He wants to restore the years that the locusts have eaten (see Jl 2:25), and He wants to give us life in abundance. But, as the Hayes' story illustrates, we must be open to receive that grace and we must choose to cooperate with it.

Conversion is not a one-time event, rather it is an ongoing process that begins afresh each day. Through the light of the Holy Spirit, God will lovingly reveal to us the aspects of our lives and hearts that need to be brought into conformity with Him. Through prayer and the sacraments, He will give us the perseverance and hope, the courage and zeal, the humility and trust true conversion requires. And, through the gift of the Holy Spirit active in our lives, God will bring to completion the good work He has begun in us (see Phil 1:6). Like Paul and Jodi we can place our confidence in that.

For videotapes featuring Dr. Paul Hayes contact

Living His Life Abundantly® International, Inc.
325 Scarlet Boulevard
Oldsmar, FL 34677-3019
(813)854-1518
or visit www.lhla.org

ELEVEN

Cancer's Hidden Grace
The Story of Dan and Bobbi Vaughan

~❧~

For as we share abundantly in Christ's sufferings, so through Christ we share abundantly in comfort too.

2 CORINTHIANS 1:5

Sometimes we find ourselves "coasting" in our relationship with the Lord. But occasionally God permits circumstances to occur in our lives that shake us from our complacency and challenge us to seek a deeper relationship with Him. Such was the case with Dan and Bobbi Vaughan, who learned through a test of faith that God is present in the midst of every event in life, and that when we unite our cross to Christ's, great joy can be found in suffering. Their story was an inspiration to me, and I hope it will be for you as well.

As Dan and Bobbi Vaughan sat across from me in the radio suite of Living His Life Abundantly®, one would never have guessed the trial they had experienced. Dan's Irish eyes danced with life and a smile played at the corners of his mouth. He seemed the picture of health. Bobbi, his wife of forty years, radiated peace and a serenity of heart that only comes from trust in God. These were no Sunday Catholics. These were Catholics of great faith, Catholics whose faith had been tested in the crucible of suffering. Catholics who had discovered a great truth—suffering can yield abundant fruit when we surrender it to the Lord.

Life was good for Dan and Bobbi Vaughan in 1988. Parents of four adult children, they were enjoying their first grandbaby and anticipating the arrival of their second. Financially they were secure. Dan's entrepreneurial spirit and astute business acumen had yielded several successful enterprises and a comfortable style of living.

They were faithful Catholics. Most mornings saw them at Mass and both prayed the rosary every day. All was near picture-perfect. The only real shadow was Dan's chronic stomach pain, which had been a fact of his life ever since he sustained serious abdominal injuries in an automobile accident when he was a young man. So, when his discomfort began to increase slightly, Dan paid little attention to it and blamed it on age.

However, around Thanksgiving, new symptoms began to develop and the tenderness between his diaphragm and stomach began to intensify. Bobbi and the children persuaded Dan to see a doctor. None of them was prepared to receive the news they heard—Dan had cancer, and needed immediate surgery to save his life.

From the onset, it seemed the hand of God guided them. A "chance" conversation of a good friend led them to the cancer specialist whose skill and ingenuity were indispensable to Dan's medical needs. Dan's and Bobbi's friend worked at a health club where the cancer specialist's wife was a patron. One morning, the doctor's wife noticed that the Vaughan's friend looked poorly. The friend had learned of Dan's illness the night before and had been so concerned for him she hadn't been able to sleep. The friend told the doctor's wife about Dan's cancer, and the doctor's wife told the friend to have Dan call her husband. She thought he'd be able to help him. Dan recalls:

*That evening we called him and [the doctor's wife] invited us over to
her home where the doctor examined me in his living room. He told
me to get my records over to his office as soon as possible, which I did
the next day. And he scheduled me for an operation ... I think it was
because the man was so experienced in the area that my problem
existed that I'm here today ... I think a lesser doctor would have simply sewn me up and told me to go home and make my final plans.*

Dan's assessment was probably right. In almost forty years of medical practice, the specialist told him he had never seen anything like he
saw in Dan the day he operated. The cancer was virulent and had
spread to many of Dan's major organs. The surgery, scheduled for
three hours, ultimately took nine and a half hours to complete. It was
rigorous, difficult, and unconventional surgery. And it was the first
time such a procedure had ever been performed.

Bobbi and family members kept vigil in the waiting room. As the
clock ticked one hour, then two, then three, and into four, the worry
and concern began to mount. Bobbi remembers:

*I was in kind of a state of semi-shock.... But when the surgery turned
out to be so long and when the doctor finally came out four and a
half hours after the surgery started and ... informed us he was only
half done, ... I just couldn't believe it. He took us into a consultation
room and diagrammed what he was doing.... Our oldest son was the
one who ... had the sense of mind to ask the doctor the questions that
needed to be asked and learn what we needed to learn.*

In that consultation, the cancer specialist told the Vaughans he was
removing Dan's entire stomach, 50 percent of his esophagus, and 25

percent of his pancreas. Through subsequent surgeries he would reroute and recreate Dan's entire digestive system. He would basically "rebuild" Dan on the inside. This was overwhelming news for the Vaughans and difficult to absorb. But, one thing was abundantly clear: Just as surely as Dan's body was being altered, so too was life as the Vaughans knew it. And, like Dan's body, many of these changes would be permanent.

Daily Graces

Dan was in the hospital for over two weeks and spent a good portion of that time in the intensive care unit. During the second week, the medical staff took Bobbi to a clinic that trained lay people in the care of the critically ill.

Bobbi's education taught her the many medical procedures she needed to know so she could care for Dan once he came home. She learned how to administer medications into a line that ran to his heart, how to clean the esophageal bag that caught his saliva, how to sterilize the ports of the tubes that carried his chemotherapy. She learned how to give him injections, how to change his dressings, how to feed him through a tube. In short, Bobbi received a crash course in nursing, and she was an apt and attentive student.

I was determined that I was going to do what I could to keep Dan from ... getting an infection. I wanted to be sure that I could do everything exactly as they told me in terms of sterilizing his ports and all these things so that he wouldn't get anything through my administrations with him. And I found out that, through the help of God, you settle into a routine. All the things that we had to do to take care of Dan just became a part of that routine.

The daily routine was made more difficult by an accident that occurred during Dan's surgery. One of his vocal chords was inadvertently severed. For over two months, at a most critical time of his recovery, he could speak only in a slight whisper. At the time, there was no guarantee that Dan's voice would ever return. Since trying to speak exhausted Dan, he and Bobbi worked out a communication system using a small school bell. Dan recalls the morning his voice came back:

I didn't know if my voice would ever come back. But, the phone rang on Easter Sunday morning and everyone was at Mass and I was the only one in the house. So ... I answered the telephone. It was an old friend of mine who was a general at a base out in Virginia. He was calling to find out how I was coming along because he had heard that I was sick. When I answered the phone I began to whisper as loud as I could and my voice came out! And that was a real miracle. It was just unbelievable that it happened on Easter Sunday morning. The sun was shining beautifully outside. It was magnificent! It was certainly a confirmation of God's presence in all of this.

This was just one of the many "God-incidences" that occurred through the course of Dan's ordeal. From a casual comment between acquaintances at a health club to regaining his voice on Easter Sunday, God was showing Dan that He was present in the midst of all of his trials and sufferings. He was showing Dan that He had a plan for him. Through these revelations, Dan's faith was growing stronger just as he was physically gaining strength a little each day.

But it was not only His love and mercy that God was revealing to Dan. God was also showing him that changes needed to be made in their relationship. At the time he was stricken with cancer, Dan had several business ventures in various stages of development. He was a key person in making this enterprise grow and prosper. But, through Dan's illness, God was showing him who really was in charge.

I had over four hundred employees for whom I was directly respon-sible in several different businesses. I was the man who was giving the orders and everybody would respond to what I requested to be done. Well, I began to realize I was not in control. There was really Somebody else up there.... And I was learning what my position was, and it wasn't the man in control.... I began to realize that God was really present in everything that I did but I wasn't giving Him the recognition.... It wasn't something that struck me like a bolt of light-ning, it was just something that gradually grew within me.

Dan realized that though he often went to daily Mass, and though he prayed the rosary every day, his business life was segregated from his life of faith. "I did Mass in the morning, and I said the rosary on the way to work in my car, but the rest of the day was about me. I wasn't bringing God into the workplace like I should have been—as much as I should have been." Dan had to reappraise his perspective of Catholicism. He had to see his faith as a dynamic meant to inform all aspects of his life. He needed to make some changes.

And still there was more that Dan began to see. He began to under-stand that the pain he was suffering could be used for a greater pur-pose. Just as Christ's sacrifice upon Calvary attained redemptive grace for Dan's salvation, so too could his pain, united to Christ's sufferings, be a source of spiritual life for others.

The pain that I had was really my prayer and I thought of pain as something I could offer up. I used that pain to remind me of God's presence in my life. He's not just there when I go to Mass in the morning. He's not just there when I say the rosary. He's there every moment ... and in everything that I do.

And, as Dan experienced, He was with him even in his pain. Bobbi was also experiencing a heightened awareness of God's presence.

One of the things that I came to realize very soon was that I could only do this one day at a time. When I tried to look down that road, I mean, I couldn't ... I couldn't do that and do the things I had to do for Dan all day every day. I had a little notebook and I had to write everything down to make sure I didn't forget something. But I decided I can do this today. And ... that was one of the greatest lessons I learned outside of the fact that God was there with me, was that if I take it one day at a time, that's all I have to do.... I don't think I really lived that way before.

God was giving Bobbi the actual grace she needed for that day. Tomorrow's grace, or the grace for next week or for next year, would come only as she needed it. He was giving her the grace she needed for the task at hand.

A Family Transformed

But as with all actual grace, it required cooperation. And, by cooperating, Bobbi found out she had more courage and perseverance than she realized. Though she had always relied on Dan's strength in crisis situations, she discovered she was much stronger and more capable than she thought. In addition to caring for Dan, many of the everyday decisions became her responsibility. She met the challenge and decided wisely. She knew this was through the inspiration of the Holy Spirit and cooperating with the grace He offered her.

But something else was happening within Bobbi. And, demonstrating courage and wisdom, she confronted it head-on. She shared:

When Dan came home from the hospital and I was taking care of him, and doing all these procedures on him, I began to notice ... I was starting to feel some resentment. I mean our lives had been turned upside down. We went from going places, doing things, out to dinner, having fun with friends to nothing but a sick person in a hospital bed. I mean I love Dan dearly and I was willing to do anything that I needed to do, but it was difficult to adjust to this life.

Bobbi's recognition and admission of her emotions were signs of her growing spiritual sensitivity. But, what she did next was a sign of her increased spiritual maturity. She took these emotions to prayer.

I think that was when my first real prayer from the heart probably came—that prayer of desperation maybe one would call it. I just said, "Lord, I know that my husband is so sick and he needs all of my love and support in order to get well, but if I start feeling resentful he will ... [sense it,] and that will not be good for either one of us. I need special grace to do this task. I need to be able to do this with love and joy."

The Lord heard and answered Bobbi's heartfelt prayer.

God gave me the greatest gift of grace and peace ... One of the things I discovered that was so amazing was that in the middle of all this anguish and suffering was this deep sense of joy. And it's not something that I ever thought could be part of pain and suffering. So now when I read in Scripture we must "pick up our cross and follow Him" ... it makes a lot of sense to me.

The misfortune of evils does not kill you but instructs you. The suffering of adversity does not degrade you but exalts you. Human tribulation teaches you; it does not destroy you.

St. Isidore of Seville

Daily, Dan and Bobbi were living out the reality of the spiritual changes taking place within them. And this witness was not lost on their children. Impressed by what they saw in their parents, they, too, began to seek a deeper relationship with the Lord. And rich spiritual fruit started to be born within the family.

The Vaughan family began to gather together for prayer, and while much of it initially centered on intercession for Dan's recovery, their prayer time soon broadened and expanded. The family added Scripture reading and discussion to their time together, sharing how particular passages applied to their individual lives and circumstances. Dan found this to be particularly helpful to him during his recovery process.

It was through the prayer and through some readings that I began to realize that this could be for the better. And I think the more we pray, the more we read the Bible, the closer we come to God, the more we come to know the truth. And the truth is God doesn't give us these things so that we can become angry, and there must be a reason for it. And I figured it had to be because God was trying to remind me that He was with me.

Eventually, a hunger to learn more about their Catholic faith sent the family searching for resources and materials that could satisfy their deepening desire to learn more about Christ and His Church. Videotapes, audiocassettes, books, and formal study materials provided the backbone for their enrichment sessions. For all of the family members, this was a time of conversion of heart and spiritual growth. Dan and Bobbi began to see that, indeed, God did have a plan in this illness, and His plan was greater than they could have imagined.

Ten months after his initial operation Dan went in for the first of two reconstructive surgeries aimed at creating a new digestive system for him. The procedure is called *colonic interposition*. In the first of these two surgeries, the doctor routed 40 percent of Dan's large intestine to a new location in his body. Making sure that its nerves and blood supply came with it, he placed the intestine over Dan's chest bone, just underneath his skin.

In time, this portion of his large intestine would become a passage-way between Dan's *jejunum* and *ileum* (the upper and lower parts of the small intestine) and what remained of his esophagus. But the graft-ing together would not take place until the second phase of recon-struction, once the doctor was certain the blood and nerve supply would keep the relocated section of large intestine alive.

Phase One was a success, and six weeks later, the second recon-structive surgery took place. The surgeon took the remainder of Dan's esophagus and routed it over his clavicle, positioning it to meet with the large intestine he had placed there in the first surgery. He then sewed together the esophagus and the large intestine at the ileosical valve. Now the route between the esophagus and the small intestine was complete. The relocated section of large intestine had replaced Dan's stomach and the 50 percent of esophagus lost to cancer. Hopefully, this would restore Dan's ability to take food through his mouth.

This second phase of the surgery took place on December 8, the Feast of the Immaculate Conception. To the joy of all, it, too, was a success. Thirteen subsequent surgical procedures over the next five months would be required to open the newly fashioned connection, but by chewing his food really well and drinking plenty of liquids with it, after sixteen months of tube feeding, Dan was finally able to take food through his mouth. Though pain from adhesions remains, Dan welcomes the twinges and stabs. *"Every time I have a sharp pain, I think of God's presence in my life, that He's always there."*

Sharing the Good News

Over the past twelve years, as a result of their experience, Dan and Bobbi have acquired a contemplative attitude toward life. Seeing God in the midst of everything, recognizing that He has a plan and purpose for each of us, knowing that He works all things to the good, and welcoming those occasions that permit us to unite our sufferings to Christ, can all be spiritually transforming events. The benefits are multiplied as this awareness is shared with others.

Dan and Bobbi make use of every opportunity to proclaim the marvelous deeds of the Lord. Evangelization has become an important part of their lives. From one-on-one evangelization to inviting young couples into their homes for faith enrichment evenings, the Vaughans seek to share with others about God's love and faithfulness. They also find themselves ministering to those who find themselves in the throes of difficult illnesses. Bobbi recounts:

Learning the great gift that suffering can bring when we abandon ourselves to God's will has given me a sense of conviction which enables me to proclaim the wonders of God to other people. But I also think ... what we went through has made me so much more aware of other people's suffering. It's made me more willing and more eager to go and support other people in their suffering and to share with them. It's amazing how our suffering opens the doors for other people.

In this way, the Vaughans have experienced the truth of 2 Corinthians 1:4-5: *"[God] comforts us in all our affliction, so that we may be able to comfort those who are in any affliction, with the comfort with which we ourselves are comforted by God. For as we share abundantly in Christ's suf-ferings, so through Christ we share abundantly in comfort too.*"

One particular endeavor has been very special to the Vaughans. Ten years ago they formed a foundation that supports a Catholic seminary in Gulu, Uganda. Through fundraising efforts, their apostolate pro-vides over 85 percent of the seminary's annual operating budget. Over the years, their funds have reroofed buildings, purchased vehicles, and helped to support the 150-165 seminarians who are in attendance at all times. The funds have also assisted seventy alumni in the major seminary as well as several priests in the archdiocese. Vocations are abundant in Africa, and Dan and Bobbi feel blessed to help nurture and support them.

Though Dan's illness prevented him from fully resuming his busi-ness endeavors, God is using all of his business acumen and gifts and talents to help build His kingdom. And for this, Dan has only grati-tude. *"The miracle wasn't really my healing, my physical healing. The miracle was my spiritual healing and the gifts that I've been given by God, and the strength that I've been given by God to carry that faith to other people."* Tested in the crucible of suffering, Dan and Bobbi's faith has become a source of faith for many others.

Heavenly Father:

Whether I am a "cradle Catholic"
or a brand-new Christian,
the process of conversion is a never-ending one.
By your Holy Spirit, show me the areas in my life that
require a change of heart, and fill me with a renewed
sense of my love for You and Your Church.
I ask this in Jesus' name, Amen.

PART FOUR

The Love of
$\mathcal{G}$od Among Us

Sharing Abundant Life With Others

Beloved, let us love one another; for love is of God, and he who loves is born of God and knows of God. He who does not love does not know God; for God is love.

1 JOHN 4:7-8

*O*ne of the most glorious (and most terrifying) images in the Gospels appears in Matthew chapter 25. Jesus uses the imagery of the shepherd and his sheep to impress upon His listeners the responsibility of believers to care for one another—and for the whole world.

Imagine how you will feel at that moment. "Come, O blessed of my Father;… I was hungry, and you gave me food,… a stranger and you welcomed me" (Mt 25:34-35).

I did? When? Grateful for what you initially suppose to be a heavenly "clerical error," you breathe a sigh of relief when the King explains. *"Truly, I say to you, as you did it to one of the least of these my brethren, you did it to me"* (v. 40).

Or imagine, just for a moment, that somehow you managed to wind up with the "goats," and heard the anguished words of the Lord, "As you did it not to one of the least of these, *you did it not to me"* (v. 45).

What would you say? What could you say?

Thankfully, every day we have another opportunity to live out the gospel in a fresh, new way. In the stories that follow, we find touching reminders of what it means to find "Jesus in distressing disguise," as Mother Teresa used to say. The hungry, the lonely, the homeless, the feeble-minded, the powerless: beloved children of God, and our brothers and sisters in Christ. Every day we have an opportunity to serve the Lord by blessing the weakest and most vulnerable members of His family.

Let the loving begin.

TWELVE

A Legacy of Love in Mexico

The Story of Maru Ahumada

Truly, I say to you, as you did it to one of the least of these my brethren, you did it to me.

MATTHEW 25:40

Hidden beneath Maru Ahumada's graceful bearing is a will of iron that has been surrendered to the Lord. And it is that combination, demonstrated in the virtues of fortitude and perseverance, which has strengthened her for her ministry to Mexico's poorest of the poor. At the time of our interview, Maru had served for more than twenty years in leper colonies and in brickyards. She had built schools and instituted health programs. She had clothed children and ministered to the outcast. She had prepared meals and catechized. She had shared joys, sorrows, sufferings, and life with those who were, in many respects, a forgotten people. Through her witness, may we all grow more certain of God's call to serve the least of His brethren.

Two dark eyes stare out of a sun-browned face and for a split second childlike wonder ignites them. The appearance of the tiny animal scurrying across his path has captured the little one's curiosity. He crouches down for a better look, but all too quickly the intruder passes, a fleeting pleasantry in the middle of a long hot day.

The six-year-old stands up and lays hold of his shovel once again. His eyes, so recently lit by curiosity and delight, return to the sun-parched earth out of which he hopes to coax a few pesos to help his family. His gaze turns desolate, like the ground he begins to strike again. He is a child of the brickyards, one of millions who live in cardboard villages throughout the country of Mexico. And like many brickyard children, he has worked this barren ground since he was four.

The occupants of the brickyards are Mexico's poorest of the poor. Our little friend is one of twenty thousand people packed together on a barren patch of earth outside of Mexico City, the largest city in the world. There, bricks are made much as they were in medieval times. Manure, water, and soil are combined, stirred by hand, poured into molds, and baked in ovens.

It is a family enterprise, this making of bricks. And it is the family's sole means of existence. Payment per brick is only a few pesos so every hand is useful. Toddlers, older children, and mothers all participate. They must work hard when they can. Rainy season is four months long. Then, the bricks do not dry and the money does not come. Hard work now can help prevent greater hunger later.

Deprivation defines life in the brickyards. There is no electricity, no plumbing, and no running water. Pollution from the ovens and disease from the squalor abound. Alcoholism is a continuing problem. The death rate is high. Government help is low.

The brickyard people are illiterate and uneducated. Most are unaccounted for in civil records. Brickyard people don't register their births or their deaths. By the world's standards, they are an unknown people, a forgotten people. But by God's standards they are His children. They deserve dignity, love, and respect. Who will carry His love to them? Who will bring them hope? Who will answer His call?

A First Impression

Maru Ahumada remembers the day she first visited the brickyards. She had been serving in a leper colony for ten years. Her life in ministry had begun as the result of a car accident. The wife of a dermatologist, and the mother of six children, Maru had been living the "good life." Golf and card playing had marked her days. Social events and parties had marked her nights. Her husband had asked her many times to visit the leper families he treated. He knew some tender loving care would be good for them. But Maru had no interest. She was too busy with her own schedule.

And then one day she was in a terrible car accident and everything changed forever. As the vehicle skidded out of control, Maru was certain she was going to die. Just before impact, she cried out to the Lord, "Please, Lord! Give me a second chance! I don't want to face you empty-handed!" Like the servant in the parable who buried his talents, Maru knew she had buried the gifts God had given to her. Now, in this moment so near to death, her hands appeared empty before her. She wanted another opportunity to use her talents to produce much for the kingdom of God. She wanted her hands to be full when she presented them to the Lord at the moment of death, not empty and wanting.

God heard her plea. Maru did not die. However, she did sustain serious injuries. Three months of bed rest followed. It was just what she needed. The Lord had Maru's undivided attention and He used this time to heal her heart as well as her body. "The Lord comforts the afflicted and afflicts the comfortable," Maru says of this time. One day, while meditating on the crucifix she kept in bed with her, Maru sensed the Lord calling her to work with the poorest of the poor. Her immediate response indicated how much interior progress had been made.

"OK, Lord," she said, "I am an available sinner. I am here to serve You. Use me."

When she had healed enough to drive, Maru set out to work with the lepers as her husband had previously suggested. She threw herself into her work and much good was accomplished. She was happy. She was peaceful. And, she was fulfilled. "You know, when you find out that the Lord really appointed you to do this kind of work, and you were lucky enough to hear that invitation and to say 'Yes, Lord,' then your life's goal seems to be exactly the same. ... My whole inner attitude changed completely."

But, one Christmas Day the Lord brought a new challenge and a new outreach to Maru. She was at the leper colony celebrating the holy day with the lepers, when she saw some people approaching the building. She couldn't believe what she was seeing:

> *They were the poorest looking persons I had ever seen in my life. Not even in magazines had I seen the sight I was seeing. It was a group of barefooted women and children ... very dirty ... coming to this leper colony to collect the leftovers of the sick persons there.*

Maru asked a social worker who these people were, and discovered they worked across the street from the leper colony in the brickyards. She knew she had to go and visit. Maru describes her first impression:

> *After I saw these people, I knew in my heart that I had to do something about them. I visited them the next week ... and what I found really made my heart cry. Really cry. I was used to poverty and I was used to misery, but I never imagined in my country there were people who were really starving to death and who would be living like*

little animals, who would not have electricity, who would not have
any services, who wouldn't even be registered for civic purposes. So
that morning, I walked and my heart was really aching, you know,
it was the kind of sadness that could really penetrate your heart.

On this preliminary trip, one of the places Maru visited was the
school. Thirty-five children (out of the fourteen thousand or so who
lived in the brickyard) were there. Their desks and chairs were pieces
of wood and bricks.

"Why are so few coming to school?" Maru asked the teacher. He
told her how hard it was to convince the parents to let the children
come to school. They would lose the child's labor for the day, he
explained. The teacher also told her that when the children did come
to school many of them fainted from hunger. Maru was quick to
respond. "You know what? I really don't know how, but in the name
of the Lord, I promise to you that we are going to do something about
this."

Later, she reflected upon that day. "I don't know who I meant when
I said that 'we' were going to help. I was by myself. But I knew the
Lord would provide...."

Maru went home and shared her experience of the day with her
husband. She was torn inside. She knew she had to do something for
these poor people of the brickyards, but she loved the people at the
leper colony very much. She knew she couldn't do both. Her husband
solved her dilemma. "You have to follow the vision," he advised. "I
think that you met these people because the Lord wanted you to leave
your already comfortable position at the leper colony." Once again,
God was afflicting the comfortable to comfort the afflicted. Maru left
the leper colony and went to the brickyards.

A New Mission

Maru shared the story of the brickyards with her friends. They had observed the changes in her life through the years and her witness had been convicting them. Perhaps they, too, needed to be doing more than golfing and playing cards. Maru encouraged them to come and join her in the brickyards, and through their efforts, much began to be accomplished. The women began by making use of what was available to them. Maru shares:

> When we started working, we decided to have a school done right away. So we chose the nearest tree and that was our first school. The one that existed for the thirty-five children attending was a grammar school. And all the toddlers were in the mud with the dogs and, you know, it was disastrous.
>
> So we started to visit the mothers. We had a megaphone and called to them. "Please come. Please come because we want to speak to you." And the women started getting together and we told them we were going to start school next week. And they kept staring at each other. "How are they going to start school?" And I said, "We have an excellent shadow in that tree there."

School began the very next week with one class under the big tree. Soon, there were classes under all the available trees. As the mothers' confidence grew so did the number of children attending Maru's school.

But the ladies soon discovered the truth of the grammar teacher's words. The children came to school hungry. They were starving. Maru found a woman who lived nearby that was willing to let them use her kitchen. They brought milk and they made the children shakes for breakfast. When so many children got sick the first day, they discovered the content was too rich. With trial and error they finally adjusted it so that the children could benefit from the nutritious breakfast milk shakes. Other changes began to take place as well. The ladies brought the authorities into the brickyards to register the children. They set up an adult education program to teach the women how to read and write. They started sewing classes and nutrition classes for the mothers, and they began to teach them how to sell their wares in the stores in Mexico City so that they would have money during the rainy season.

One immediate priority was to teach the people the Word of God. The ladies found the women and children to be apt and eager students and soon they started to bring their husbands and fathers with them. The ladies prepared the children for First Holy Communion and the parents for the Sacrament of Matrimony. The need for birth certificates and other papers had made it difficult for the men and women to marry in the past, but Maru and her women were helping all of this to be accomplished.

Other people also helped. Maru organized a group of women to help from their homes. They collected communion dresses for the girls and communion outfits for the boys. Some baked cakes, others raised donations, and still others wrote thank-you notes. A strong outside contingency of help continues to aid Maru and the ladies in their work.

New Helpers in the Mission

The brickyards were being transformed. Maru and her ladies worked daily and diligently to improve the living conditions, lifestyle, and environment of the brickyard people. Their educational outreach was a big success and soon, there simply were not enough trees. A building was needed. So, Maru visited the governor of the state. She told him about the conditions in the brickyard, the work she and her ladies had been doing, and the needs they now had. He sent a representative and, upon inspection, the state began to plan a school building for the brickyards.

Maru was quick to give the requirements for the new building. "We needed a huge kitchen, and we needed a dining room where we could serve the children. And we told him we planned to serve them both breakfast and lunch." The representative assured Maru that this was not possible. There was no way the state could feed all of the children. It would deplete their resources too rapidly.

In typical fashion, Maru responded with faith and trust in God. She told him, "We are not asking for that. We want the physical building. We will do the rest. And we'll take care of the teachers and we will pay the teachers." Maru had no idea how she and her ladies would manage what she had just promised, but she was certain God had a plan. "It's so much fun to watch the Lord in action because He is the best inventor in the world!"

Not long after, it became apparent that a new grammar school was necessary. This time, Maru visited the governor's wife. She told her the story of the brickyards and the desperate need they had for a new school, and then Maru invited her to come and visit. The governor's wife agreed. She arrived by helicopter and was deeply moved by what she saw. She promised Maru she would do her best to help.

And she kept her word. The two-classroom schoolhouse that once served the brickyards gave way to a six-classroom school, which was eventually expanded to nine classrooms. While the old school had no bathrooms, the new building was equipped with six, two for the teachers and four for the children. A play area was built for the children complete with a soccer field and a basketball court.

But Maru's vision was not complete. A technical high school was needed for the older children. She believed that if they could be trained in the trades they could break the cycle of poverty their families had known for generations. She explains,

> *We have all the reason in the world to believe that the children that have accomplished something in life—they know how to read and write, they know how to add—they will have a better opportunity in life.... The technical high school [would] give them a little certificate and they [could] work at plumbing, carpentry, and the girls [could] learn how to make dresses. They can go to factories and work. And the whole idea is really to take these people out of the slavery work they have to do.*

For this, Maru needed big help and big money.

It is from the love of God that Christians learn to help the needy and to share with them their own material and spiritual goods. Such concern not only provides those experiencing hardship with material help but also represents an opportunity for the spiritual growth of the giver, who finds in it an incentive to become detached from worldly goods.

Pope John Paul II

Our Lady of Guadalupe: Mother of the Brickyards

Maru had always dedicated the work of the brickyards to Our Lady of Guadalupe, Patroness of Mexico and Patroness of the Americas. And she always sought Our Lady's intercession each step of the way. Pictures of her had been hung in the schools. The children had all learned about her apparitions to Juan Diego in 1531, and the favors and blessings that came from them. They heard the story of the tilma, Juan Diego's apron, upon which Our Lady had miraculously imprinted her image. And they learned about the great basilica in Mexico City, erected in her honor, where hung Our Lady's image still brilliant and lovely after all these hundreds of years.

Maru has always had a deep devotion to Our Lady of Guadalupe and she believes that Our Lady of Guadalupe is especially interested in the poorest of the poor. So when she was asked to speak about her to a group of people in Philadelphia, Pennsylvania, she accepted the invitation. Little did she know what Our Lady had planned for her.

Maru gave her presentation and at the very end she used the brickyards as an illustration of what can happen through Our Lady of Guadalupe's intercession. Following the talk, a gentleman approached Maru and asked her to come to his home to meet his wife and talk with them about her work. Maru sensed the importance of this opportunity. She recalls,

I asked the assistance of the Holy Spirit because I really needed to be very inspired. I knew that something was going on because Our Lady was in action. So I took my time to let him know what we had discovered, what we were doing, our immediate plans, our plans for the future.

Obviously impressed, the gentleman asked Maru how much money she needed. Maru wasn't sure how to respond but once again the Holy Spirit came to her aid. She invited him to come and visit. He agreed, and two months later he was in Mexico City being chauffeured by Maru to the brickyards. She took him to all the sites. She took him to the schools. She showed him the brick-making process. She had him visit with the brickyard people in their homes. And, when all was said and done, he gave her a gift of $750,000. With it Maru built two schools—a new grammar school and the technical high school she so wanted for the older children.

A Legacy of Love

Maru and her ladies have accomplished much in the brickyards outside of Mexico City. Nineteen hundred children are educated in the six schools they have built. They serve twenty-six hundred meals every day through the schools' breakfast and lunch programs. They have instituted adult education programs. They provide catechetical instruction and preparation for the Sacraments. They teach basic nutrition and health care. They have established a clinic with free medicine and a full-time doctor.

But most importantly, they have brought to the brickyards the love of God. It is this that the people feel, it is this to which they respond, and it is this that is changing their lives. Maru and her ladies not only tell the brickyard people about the love of God, they live the love of God. And that is what makes all the difference.

With a smile lit by grace, Maru states,

I'm not pretending that my hands are full, but you know they are not as empty as they were, and I am aware of the fact that as long as I live and have the energy, I'm here to serve the Lord. I am at His disposal.

Maru and her ladies show us what can happen when we respond to God's call. Our lives are filled with many opportunities to be ambassadors of God's love by giving of ourselves. But, we often miss the challenge. It is not that we intend to be uncharitable. It is simply that we have done little to cultivate a "charitable outlook" which helps us see the corporal and spiritual needs of our neighbor.

Let us ask God to give us a "vision of mercy" that enables us to recognize the needs of others. And let us ask Him to increase our trust, relying on His grace to accomplish all He desires us to do. In this way, like Maru and her ladies, we will ignite the fire of divine love in all whom we meet.

THIRTEEN

The Woman Loved Into Life
The Story of "Muriel"

᰾

*I want to know Christ and the power of his resurrection and the
sharing of his sufferings by becoming like him in his death, if
somehow I may attain the resurrection from the dead.*

PHILIPPIANS 3:10-11, NRSV

*What does the Resurrection of Jesus mean to us? To what extent does
it influence the way we think—about ourselves, our relationship
with God, eternity, our interactions with others?*

*Do we see it as a singular historical moment, or do we see it as
an event with eternal implications—a God-powered event meant to
empower each one of us? When we contemplate the Resurrection of
Jesus Christ from the perspective of faith, we may find that we are
forever transformed by our pondering.*

*Here is a true story that resonates with Resurrection power. It is
about a few people who dared to believe the same power that raised
Jesus Christ from the dead is a living reality that can imbue even the
bleakest situation with new life. Let's meet Cathy, Muriel, Maureen,
and Marty.*

When Cathy first saw Muriel, she found the older woman
reclining in a special chair in the nursing home. A faded
housedress covered Muriel's slight frame, and a white institutional
blanket concealed her legs. Muriel's long gray hair was brushed straight
back. Her eyes were closed tight and her mouth hung open in a wide

lifeless gape. She was pale and blotchy. Sunshine had not reached her in a long time.

Muriel was a stroke victim. She had been in the nursing home for seven years. She had been her husband's caretaker during the years he battled Parkinson's disease. When Muriel suffered the stroke it took him forty-five long minutes to get her help.

It was because of her husband's disease that many people questioned his judgment when he signed for her feeding tube. Most thought Muriel would be better off dead. But he insisted she be given food and water. And because of his decision, Muriel had outlived him.

She wasn't alone in the world, however. She had a son and a daughter. But they lived far away and only came to see her every year or two. Cathy's aunt was Muriel's friend. When she told Cathy about Muriel's situation, Cathy decided to pay this woman a visit.

Now Cathy stood facing Muriel, not really knowing what to do or what to say now that her "good intention" had taken on flesh. "Hello. I'm Cathy," she began. "I'm the niece of your friend. I thought I'd come by and spend some time with you."

Cathy's greeting received no response. Of course, what did she think Muriel would do? It was plain to see that she was extremely debilitated. Her hands were clenched tightly—so tightly that her knuckles had given out long ago and her fingers curled back upon themselves. Clearly, she hadn't moved in a long time.

Cathy felt awkward. Beyond her greeting, she didn't know what to say to Muriel. In fact, she wasn't even sure if Muriel wanted her there. So mostly Cathy just sat quietly, watching the hands of the clock move by, the uncomfortable silence broken only by the nursing aides who occasionally came into the room.

It was clear the aides weren't doing much for Muriel beyond what they had to do. Muriel's personal hygiene, and Cathy's nose, said as much. In addition, Cathy was disturbed by the way the aides treated Muriel, as though she was a piece of furniture. Pushed her here. Moved her there. And no one talked to Muriel directly. Instead, they talked about her in the third person—as if she couldn't hear. As if she were dead already. All of this bothered Cathy considerably.

When it was time to go, Cathy told Muriel she would be back to see her again. Her heart ached for this woman who seemed frozen in time. She wanted to do something for her, but what? She couldn't even communicate with her or get a reaction from her.

A Plan of Action

Though Cathy left Muriel, Muriel didn't leave Cathy. She was constantly in her thoughts. How could Cathy help her? What was God asking her to do? Cathy found the answer during her prayer time. Cathy saw Muriel for the person God created her to be: His precious daughter, whom He loved infinitely and completely. And God's love for Muriel poured into Cathy's heart.

Now she understood what it was that troubled her about the attitude of the aides—they didn't treat Muriel as a person, someone uniquely and individually created by God. Rather, they seemed to measure her worth by her present physical condition. And in that evaluation, Muriel came up short.

In prayer, Cathy saw Muriel's debilitation as the cross of Christ. Cathy knew that Muriel had been a daily communicant when she was well. She began to see that Eucharistic grace filled her heart. Muriel *was* suffering. But her suffering was not without purpose. It was redemptive. And Cathy knew that redemption leads to resurrection.

At last, Cathy knew how to relate to Muriel. She was a child of God. That's who Muriel was and that's how Cathy would treat her. The next time Cathy went to the nursing home, she arrived with love in her heart and books in her arms. "Hello, Muriel. I'm Cathy. Remember me? I've come to visit with you today. Do you like to read, Muriel? I hope so. I've brought some books about the lives of the saints. Here's a good one. Let's begin."

Cathy read to Muriel for a long time. The story was one about struggle and victory, the cost of discipleship and the immeasurable worth of God's love. At one point, Cathy was overwhelmed with emotion. It was a sad moment in the life of the saint she was reading about. The saint was experiencing a time of rejection and misunderstanding by those she loved most, her own family. Cathy's voice broke and she had to stop. "I'm sorry, Muriel. It's so sad," Cathy choked.

With that, she lifted her head to look up at Muriel. To her surprise, she saw a tear trickling down Muriel's cheek. "Oh, Muriel. You *do* hear and you *can* react. We can communicate, Muriel! Isn't it wonderful? Thank you, Lord, for showing me Muriel knows I'm here for her."

From that moment forward, Cathy and Muriel became the best of friends. Through the days and weeks that followed, Cathy saw more and more of Muriel's tender heart, her love of God, and how she used the gift of her suffering for the conversion of sinners. Cathy began to see the grace of abandonment at work in the soul of Muriel. They spoke to each other in the most precious of ways—heart to heart, soul to soul.

New Life

Cathy began to notice subtle nuances in Muriel's reactions when she spoke to her: the flutter of an eyelid, the movement of her toes, tiny furrows in her brow. Soon, Cathy could "read" Muriel's responses and knew what she was thinking and feeling. Often Cathy would exercise Muriel's arms and legs, coaxing life back into her limbs with gentle insistence. She made a game of it and Muriel seemed to like it.

Let us love. Let our souls and our lives be a perpetual song of love for God first of all and for all human beings who suffer, love, and mourn.

Elisabeth Leseur

Many times they prayed the rosary together, Cathy leading and Muriel "responding." Cathy would hold the crucifix to Muriel's gaping mouth and would tell her, "Kiss the crucifix, Muriel. Jesus loves you and so do I." And Muriel would twist her lips and contort them into a pucker as the wood pressed against her mouth. In time, she even began to make the Sign of the Cross. Her arm was shaky and her hand didn't quite make it to the designated places, but it was made with love and faith.

Once, Cathy had to leave the area for an extended time. She laid her head on Muriel's shoulder, kissed her cheek, and said good-bye. Muriel lifted her right arm and embraced Cathy while a tear rolled down her cheek.

Cathy asked a trusted friend and her husband to visit Muriel in her absence. Maureen and Marty followed through on their promise. They spent hours with Muriel, talking to her, praying with her, exercising her hands, and bringing small gifts. Soon they loved Muriel as much as Cathy did.

And love had its effect—Muriel began to smile—somewhat twisted and contorted, but a smile nonetheless. Whenever Marty or Maureen would mention Cathy's name, Muriel would get excited and breathe more rapidly.

By the time Cathy returned to the area, a chapel had been built in the nursing home. Every Thursday she and Maureen took Muriel to Mass. This was a special time for them and the Eucharist became the cord of grace that bound them together in love.

Often, Cathy would take Muriel to the chapel in the middle of the day. Sometimes Maureen would join them. They would sit before the tabernacle—three sisters in the Lord united by the real presence of Jesus Christ.

Father Mike, the hospital chaplain, became a frequent visitor to Muriel's room. Love radiated from that tiny space and others were drawn by it. Some of the more ambulatory residents would come out into the hall whenever Muriel was around. A sense of peace and hope seemed to accompany her.

Resurrection Power

One day Cathy arrived at the nursing home to find Muriel's room stripped of her belongings. The bed was freshly made, the dresser stark and bare, and Muriel was nowhere to be seen. Cathy discovered

Muriel's possessions stuffed into garbage bags in the corner of the room.

Fear gripped Cathy's heart. The nurse on duty told her that Muriel had been taken to the hospital the night before. She had aspirated and her lungs were filled with fluid.

When Cathy got to the hospital it was clear that Muriel was dying. Cathy called Maureen and Marty, and then she called Muriel's daughter. The daughter expressed gratitude that Cathy was there, but told her she couldn't make it. Would Cathy please take care of the arrangements?

And so it was that in her final hours, Muriel was surrounded by those faithful few who had come to love her most—Cathy, Maureen, and Marty. They gathered around her bed. They sang hymns, prayed the rosary, and encouraged her through her letting go. Father Mike came and administered the Anointing of the Sick.

Cathy and Maureen prayed the Chaplet of Divine Mercy, and as they completed it, Muriel completed her life on earth. In the solitude of a quiet place, made holy through prayer and love, a gentle soul beheld her Lord face-to-face and moved on to accept everlasting life.

It was following Muriel's death that her friends became most aware of her influence in their lives. Through their own act of charity, they had become richly blessed. In Muriel they had seen the suffering Christ. Through her silent tutelage they had learned about patient endurance. In her humility, she had taught them about true joy. She had shown them how the power of the Resurrection is released in our lives when we accept the grace of the present moment. She had shown them that through the love of God death is transformed into new life.

FOURTEEN

Abortion's Aftermath: From Trauma to Triumph

The Story of Theresa Burke and Rachel's Vineyard

~✤~

I will lead her into the desert and speak tenderly to her. There I will give her back her vineyards, and transform her Valley of Troubles into a Door of Hope.

Adapted From HOSEA 2:16-17

Living His Life Abundantly® has produced numbers of programs through the years on pro-life issues. These programs are vital to our listening and viewing audiences because they present Catholic teaching on these important topics. Of our pro-life programming, however, few touch my heart more than those programs dealing with post-abortive women. For them, abortion is not a "political issue," nor is it a matter of "women's rights." For them, abortion has become a deeply personal experience, filled with intense emotional, psychological, and spiritual suffering. In the following account, you will meet some of the women who have experienced this trauma.

The young woman sat quietly before me, her face etched with determination. Though she had shared her story many times, she had never broadcast it before. But she was resolved to take advantage of every opportunity to proclaim the truth.

We used only her first name. Her counselors thought it best. So did I. The point of the interview was not so much about her identity, but about her experience, an experience shared by approximately four thousand other women every day throughout the United States.

As Donna answered my questions, I wondered how many listening to our radio program that day found themselves in her story. How many of them could relate her details to their own life experiences? How many had made the same decision she had made—a life-changing choice formulated out of compromise and quiet desperation? I could only guess, but I knew the number had to be large.

Donna was nineteen years old when it happened, she told me. Her boyfriend was older and in the middle of a legal separation from his wife. He promised her he would seek a divorce and then marry her. They talked about their future together, a future that would include children and maybe a little girl who would look just like her.

They were in love, so when Donna discovered she was pregnant, she thought it would simply hasten the divorce and they could begin to live the dreams they had spun. But her boyfriend was not happy. He threatened to leave her. He didn't want to have anything to do with her. And he didn't want the child. Donna was shocked. They had been together for a year and a half already. What would she do?

Donna spoke with her mother, who told her that what she carried in her womb was only a blob of tissue. It wouldn't become a baby for three months. Donna hadn't considered abortion before the conversation, but now—could this be an alternative for her? She was torn. Donna desperately wanted her relationship to work, and, if all she carried was a blob of tissue, why not? But, she had to do it before the three months were up.

Abortion day arrived. Possibly the same determination I saw in her had etched her face that day, too. Donna told me she walked into the clinic focused on the fact that this was what she had to do and that she had to "get it over with." However, for a brief moment, her resolve was shattered. Her boyfriend was with her and she sat on his lap cradled like a baby. Tears began to roll down her cheeks and she pleaded with him, "Please don't make me do this! Please don't make me do this!" There was no response.

The nurse walked into the waiting room and called Donna's name. The decision was made. The die had been cast. She stood up, shoved her feelings aside, and moved through the door, shutting out emotion and sealing in denial.

Donna recalls waking up in recovery, feeling repulsed by what she saw and heard. Other women were in the room with her. They, too, had chosen abortion as the way out. Some were getting sick. Some were crying. She was disgusted with them and with herself. She couldn't deal with the sights, sounds, or the emotions. She had to leave. She had to get out of there, and fast.

Defying the thirty-minute post-op rule, she walked out. The nurse advised her to take it easy and to rest for a day or two. She shrugged off the advice. "Nothing happened. I didn't do anything. Why should I rest?" Instead, she asked her boyfriend to take her out to eat.

For a year and a half, Donna maintained her denial. And then it happened again. She was pregnant a second time by the same man. But this time she knew she wouldn't abort. She couldn't do that again. Was she emerging from her denial? Perhaps. But Donna miscarried, and that set her back. Losing the baby seemed a sweet justice. After what she had done, she felt she didn't deserve to have a child.

Another year and a half went by. This time a new man was in Donna's life. He was very nice and very principled. A minister. Yet she couldn't be with him. After their first date and a bottle of wine, she fled to her car and sobbed. He had tried to kiss her. How could she let him? He was a good man, and she—what was she? She—she was a *murderer!*

The word crashed into her consciousness. *Murderer ... murderer ... What have I done? What could I have been thinking?!* These thoughts had haunted her, flitting ghostlike in her mind, luring her to think about her actions that day. In the past she had always been able to bury them. Shove them down. Repress them. Now, however, in a moment of emotional vulnerability, her thoughts had taken on flesh and blood. She could no longer deny the truth of it. She had aborted her *baby*, not a *blob of tissue*. What would she do?

Donna had to seek reconciliation—with God, with her child, with herself. How to do it? She went to confession. And her penance was to volunteer in a crisis pregnancy center. Her search for such a ministry led her to Kimberly Home, an apostolate that provides counseling for women in crisis pregnancies or who are post-abortive. It proved a perfect match. Not only could Donna help others, but she could get the help she needed as well.

She was healing, she told me. The radio interview was taking her another step closer. She would heal, but she would never forget. And her memory, she hoped, would be a beacon of truth lighting the way for so many others lost in the darkness of their decision.

A Sisterhood of Suffering

Though the particular circumstances of my guest's experience are unique and individual, her story parallels many others. Consider these comments made by other post-abortive women:

> *I suffer from the internal wounds that pierced my heart that day sixteen years ago when I chose to abort my baby.... There were so many*

things I was not informed about, especially, the long lasting emotional and spiritual effects. ... When the reality of what I had done sunk in, I turned to alcohol and drugs to ease the pain. ... The guilt, shame, sorrow, and regret created a great "black hole" inside myself. ... For the next sixteen years I felt isolated, depressed, and anxious. ... I sought out only abusive relationships thinking I didn't deserve love, honor, or respect. – Jennifer

Painfully and slowly, I dressed and walked into the waiting room. ... I was at the end of the road. ... I had finally struck bottom. With quiet deliberation, I took my handgun from under my pillow, checking to make sure the clip was loaded. I chambered a round, walked into my living room, sat in a chair, put the gun to my head, and pulled the trigger. To this day, I cannot think why the gun did not fire.... Still numb, I called my only friend, S., and told her what I tried to do ... She was there in only a few minutes. ... She put me on her lap like I was a child and rocked me a long time. – Connie

I had an abortion because I was afraid, ignorant, alone, and confused. That one cold day in February changed the rest of my life. ... It has since been a life filled with guilt and shame. ... I think of my whole life in terms of before and after the abortion. ... The past two years have been a trip to hell and back. There have been times on this trip that suicide seemed like the best way out. ... It is a never-ending struggle, which at times I've thought I might lose. — Mary

Abortion: The Facts Behind the Faces

Legal in all fifty states through all nine months of pregnancy, abortion on demand has become a nationally protected right for women. By age forty-five, 43 percent of women in the United States have had at least one abortion. Touted as safe and often psychologically beneficial, almost three generations of women have aborted their children at an accelerating rate. At the time of this writing, over 1.4 million babies die at the hands of abortionists every year. That's four thousand babies per day.

But what of the claims of abortion advocates? Is abortion safe? Is it psychologically beneficial?

The number of potential physical complications associated with induced abortion are staggering. David Reardon, a guest whom I interviewed for both television and radio, is a biomedical ethicist and director of the Elliot Institute. The Elliot Institute performs original research and education on abortion's impact. Its website (www.afterabortion.info) states there are over one hundred potential physical complications for abortion. The following nine are the most common *major* complications: infection, excessive bleeding, embolism, ripping or perforation of the uterus, anesthesia complications, convulsions, hemorrhage, cervical injury, and endotoxic shock.

And what of the psychological effects of abortion? Women who have had post-abortion counseling report over one hundred major reactions. These include depression, loss of self-esteem, self-destructive behavior including thoughts of suicide and suicide attempts, sleep disorders, memory loss, sexual dysfunction, chronic problems with relationships, personality changes, anxiety attacks, guilt, remorse, difficulty grieving, increased tendency toward violence, chronic crying, concentration problems, flashbacks, and difficulty bonding with subsequent children.

Psychologists and mental health counselors who work with post-abortive women report that the trauma experienced by them is similar to, if not the same as, Post-Traumatic Stress Disorder (PTSD). In fact, they have named it Post-Abortion Stress or Post-Abortion Trauma. PTSD is a psychological dysfunction resulting from a traumatic experience through which a person's normal defense mechanisms are overwhelmed. Many women who have had abortions experience the symptoms of this disorder, including psychological problems, emotional struggles, and certain compulsive behavioral patterns.

A Deadly Cycle

One particularly distressing characteristic of Post-Traumatic Stress Disorder prevalent in post-abortive women is *traumatic reenactment.* Theresa Karminski Burke, Ph.D., is the founder and director of Rachel's Vineyard, a counseling ministry for post-abortive healing. She explains traumatic reenactment:

You keep putting yourself in other situations where you are likely to experience the same feelings [that you had at the time of the trauma]. Whatever the feeling was that accompanies the trauma at the time that it happened, whether it was a sense of helplessness, or violation, or extreme shame and guilt, whatever the feeling was is what you are likely to see reproduced throughout the life....

For many post-abortive women, traumatic reenactment is typified by repeat abortions. Forty-six percent of all abortions in the United States are repeat procedures. For these women, their first abortion began a painful and horrible cycle. Dr. Burke believes that "by helping to heal women suffering the trauma and grief due to abortions, we can tremendously reduce the one-and-a-half million abortions annually in the United States."

With so many potential physical and emotional complications one would expect the number of women seeking abortions to decrease rather than increase, even in a culture that offers abortion as a quick fix to a crisis pregnancy. However, time and again, women report that the potential for complications is never discussed with them. One post-abortive woman states:

> *The lies have affected me the most: the Big Lie that it all is, and all the tangled webs of lies that make it up, compromise to cover it up. The truth is that I have been affected; one of the lies is that you just move on unaffected. My heart turned cold. I just strived to survive in an empty existence—not a true life. I pretended I wasn't hurt but I was terribly so.*

Even with this much known about the potential psychological effects of abortion, a bias against diagnosing Post-Abortion Trauma is prevalent within the mental health community. In a radio program that we produced on the issue, Dr. Burke told me when she first encountered the professional bias.

During her graduate studies, she worked with women suffering from anorexia nervosa and bulimia. One night during her weekly support group, a woman shared about her abortion experience and the recurring nightmares she had about her aborted baby. Her guilt was exacerbated by messages her ex-husband left on her answering machine. In them, he called her a murderer.

The group's reaction to this woman's experience was explosive. One woman fled the room in tears. Another member angrily jumped to her feet and began to rant and to curse the woman's ex-husband. The rest simply sat with stunned or pained expressions on their faces. Dr. Burke worked to restore equilibrium to the session, and soon discovered that a good majority of the women in her group had had abortions.

This finding intrigued her. Could these women's eating disorders be symptomatic of Post-Abortion Trauma? Dr. Burke wanted to study the possible connection more closely and consulted her supervisor, a psychiatrist. His response stunned her. He flatly denied her the opportunity, insisting that she had no business "prying" into group members' abortions during sessions.

Dr. Burke learned that most mental health organizations in the United States, including the American Psychiatric Association, the National Association of Social Workers, and the American Medical Association, support abortion rights and discount the existence of Post-Abortion Trauma. Dr. Burke explains the devastating effect this has on post-abortive women:

I can't tell you how many women have come to me after having been to maybe twenty therapists ... really suffering severe things that no one is willing to recognize ... And so, behind the fence of "personal private decision" is immense suffering that no one can talk about. It is not validated by society and so it leaves a woman feeling pretty crazy. ... And anyone that is in the field, anyone that is involved in post abortion ministry sees it and there's such a great need.

From this group experience, Theresa determined that she wanted to use her professional expertise to help women suffering from Post-

Abortion Trauma. She believed that what she saw in her group members that night was a microcosm of the post-abortion population. Some cope with the injury they have sustained by talking about it, others flee from any discussion because the pain is so deep, and still others protect themselves through a defensive wall of hostility and anger. According to Dr. Burke, all of these responses render abortion a "forbidden grief." She explains,

> *For many, the secret of abortion is locked tightly in the deep recesses of the heart, admitted to no one for fear of judgment. Like the leper who cringes from the sunlight, a wounded heart seeks solace in the dark.*

Trust the past to the Mercy of God, the present to His Love, and the future to His Providence.

St. Augustine

Rachel's Vineyard: A Way of Healing

How, then, does the healing process begin? Dr. Burke states that the first step is getting a woman to talk about her experience. But this is not always easy. "The wounded spirit of one who has experienced abortion vacillates between longing for reconciliation and the despair of condemnation," says Burke. She urges those who hear the words, "I had an abortion" to be sensitive and to realize how painful those words are to speak.

Through Rachel's Vineyard, an outreach program Dr. Burke founded in 1995, women who have experienced the pain of aborting a child find a loving environment in which they can speak those words without fear of judgment or condemnation. Each year they schedule dozens of retreats all over the country for women desperate to find help from the trauma produced by the abortion experience.

The weekends are mostly attended by women who have had an abortion. However, anyone who has experienced the trauma of abortion is welcome to attend. Doctors and nurses who have performed or assisted in abortions, husbands and boyfriends who have insisted on an abortion, mothers and fathers who have encouraged their daughters to obtain an abortion often attend the retreat weekend.

Participants are gently encouraged to exercise their faith to receive the wholeness they seek. A unique concept called "Living Scripture" helps them to integrate the psychological and the spiritual. By reenacting bible stories, the emotional scars and spiritual wounds of the participants are touched by the healing love of Jesus Christ, and they come to see that there is hope. The following comments are typical of the women who have experienced Rachel's Vineyard:

I experienced Our Lord's healing touch through Rachel's Vineyard's team of support. With the help of some wonderful priests and post-abortive women who had healed their wounds, I began my journey back to God. – Jennifer

I cannot describe the healing I have received from being present at that wonderful retreat. Thanks to Rachel's Vineyard retreat, I can look in the mirror without hating the reflection I used to see. Thanks to the wonderful counselors on that retreat, I can say "I am healed, I am loved, I am saved by my Redeemer and truly know it." – Connie

I went through so many different feelings in three short days but I did not go through anything alone that weekend. There was always someone there with a hug or the words I needed to hear. ... The most wonderful thing happened on Saturday night during one of the exercises. [In prayer] I was able to see my daughter in heaven with Jesus. I finally understood that she did not hate me. Knowing this took a great weight off of me and opened the door to forgiving myself. This allows a space in my heart for hope to grow. – Mary

Each year, Rachel's Vineyard, and many other post-abortion ministries, provide a space for hope to grow in the hearts of hundreds of women. Though healing from the trauma of abortion is a heart-wrenching and painful process, healing is possible. And when it occurs, lives and souls are saved.

Are You Suffering From Post-Abortion Stress?

If you have had an abortion(s), you may be suffering from Post-Abortion Stress. Answering the following questions can help you figure out how the abortion(s) may have affected your life.

- Do you find yourself struggling to turn off feelings or memories related to your abortion(s)?
- Do you become uncomfortable around reminders of the abortion:

babies, pregnant women, doctor's offices, news reports about abortion?

- Do you feel anxious at the idea of telling a loved one about your abortion? Does it make you feel anger, sorrow, grief, or guilt?
- Do you have trouble talking about the abortion issue as a political issue?
- Are you afraid that you, your loved ones, or your other children will be hurt or killed? Are you overly protective of your children?
- Do you look at life in terms of "before" and "after" the abortion(s)? Do you become angry or depressed more easily?
- Have you experienced "reconnectors" to your abortion, such as nightmares, flashbacks, or hallucinations, such as hearing a baby cry?
- Did you use or increase your use of alcohol or drugs (illegal or prescription) after your abortion?
- Have you experienced suicidal thoughts? Do you take risks that put your life in danger? Do you try to hurt yourself? Have you developed any eating disorders?
- Have you lost interest in taking care of yourself?
- Do you have trouble with finding or maintaining good relationships with men? Do you have issues with trust and control? Do you get involved in hurtful or abusive relationships?
- Have you become promiscuous?
- Have you lost your faith? Have you lost a sense of God's peace? Do you think God still loves you?

If you are experiencing any of the above problems, post-abortion counseling may help. Skilled and understanding people want to help. Many have been through the same things you are going through now.

If you or someone you know would like more information about Rachel's Vineyard Ministries, you may contact them through their website: www.rachelsvineyard.org, or receive their toll-free number through directory assistance.

For videotapes and audiocassettes featuring Theresa Burke, Ph.D. and David Reardon contact:

Living His Life Abundantly® International, Inc.
325 Scarlet Blvd.
Oldsmar, FL 34677 -3019 or visit
www.lhla.org

The first-person accounts in this story were used with the permission of Rachel's Vineyard, **www.rachelsvineyard.org**. Facts and statistics were taken from www.afterabortion.info, the website of the Elliot Institute, and www.afterabortion.com.

FIFTEEN

Living the Love of God
The Story of Paco and Marie Colón

∼❊∽

Let brotherly love continue. Do not neglect to show hospitality to strangers, for thereby some have entertained angels unawares.

HEBREWS 13:1-2

Some time ago I produced a television program called "From Tragedy to Triumph." It featured individuals who had overcome tremendous obstacles in their lives through the help of others. It was my great pleasure to include a woman who had become my friend. Marie Colón was known in her community for helping many people in many different ways. Here is her story and the stories of some of the people she and her family have assisted.

I first met Marie Colón while working on a four-hour television documentary called "River of Light." The project traced the evangelization of Spain and the role of Our Lady of Guadalupe. Marie was playing a most important part in the production—she was raising the money. As associate producer for the project, I had to interact with Marie regularly. She was in Louisiana and I was in Florida, so we communicated primarily over the telephone. However, as the project progressed, details demanded that we meet.

Marie arrived in Clearwater, Florida, one sunny spring day. I liked her almost immediately. She was warm and engaging, and though it was our first meeting, it seemed we had known each other a long time. I was struck first and foremost by her obvious love of the Lord. It was clear to me that she was a woman of prayer—her manner and demeanor said as much. There was a certain tranquility of spirit that radiated from her. I was also impressed by her confidence in God. Though the cost of production was high, she seemed certain that the finances would come. "After all, it is God's project," she said. "We are just the poor instruments He is using to get it done."

As we visited together, I discovered that Marie and I had much in common. We were both passionate about our Catholic faith, we were both involved in evangelization though in different ways, and we were both devoted to the Blessed Mother. These commonalities made for a communication of the heart as well as of the mind.

In addition, though Marie was born in San Juan, Puerto Rico, and I was born in Pittsburgh, Pennsylvania, many of our life experiences were similar. This too, added to the bonding. Finally, we had children that were all in the same age range. Her four and my three were like chronological steps in their years of birth. As mothers, we had much to discuss. A friendship began to blossom.

The project soon took me to New Orleans, Louisiana, to participate in a Marian Conference. I was to give a talk to the main assembly about Our Lady of Guadalupe and to interest the conference participants in the production. Marie insisted that I stay at her home. When I arrived, I discovered that I was not the only conference speaker who would be staying at *Casa de Colón*. There were three of us, plus Marie's family, a few of the children's friends, and Marie's parents who were visiting from Puerto Rico. It made for a full house. The home was large and comfortable, so accommodations were no problem. But still,

I was struck by such an obvious display of hospitality and generosity. I would soon learn that these were virtues practiced again and again by my Puerto Rican friend.

In time, I learned that Marie and her husband, Dr. Francisco "Paco" Colón, regularly opened their home to guests. These guests came from a variety of backgrounds, and with a variety of needs and problems. Some were sick, confused, and forsaken. Some came disabled, depressed, and discouraged. But every person was met with compassion, hospitality, and generosity. Marie thinks of her home as God's home. "Our home belongs to God, and He brings to us the people He wants to live there for as long as He wants them there."

And God did bring them to the Colóns. For example, one family friend had brain surgery to remove a tumor, and needed around-the-clock care. Marie and Paco offered him a bedroom in their home that had an adjoining bathroom. It was a good arrangement for the recuperating friend and Marie was home to help him through the day. Along with his wife, she nursed him back to health. He was with the Colóns for several months. Marie recalls, "It was a time of great spiritual blessings and favors. God was abundantly present."

Then, there was Henry from Columbia. A priest had brought him to the Colón home after finding Henry begging for money in the French Quarter. Henry had been making his way north from Columbia through Mexico into the United States. He hopped on the roof of a train, counting on the iron rails to take him to a new and better life. Then disaster struck. Henry fell off of the train and it ran over him, severing an arm, a leg, and other parts of his body. Miraculously, he survived.

It was the priest's hope that he could help Henry acquire prosthetics so that he could gain employment and achieve the new life he so desperately wanted. But Henry needed a place to stay. Immediately, the priest thought of Marie. "Of course, of course," was Marie's response. "Bring him."

This is the true reason for our existence: to be the sunshine of God's love, to be the hope of eternal happiness. That's all.

Mother Teresa of Calcutta

Henry arrived at the Colón home with nothing but the clothes on his back. He stayed with Marie and her family for six months. During that time, Marie, Paco, and a domestic helper assisted Henry with all of his daily needs. And, Marie took him everywhere she went: the grocery store, doctor's appointments, and social gatherings. He went to daily Mass, prayer meetings, and devotions. He visited the sick, the elderly, and the homebound. For all six months, Henry was Marie's constant companion. She explains,

> I only ever have one condition—that they go with me everywhere. I want them to experience what the life of faith is all about. I want them to have a spiritual life, a family life, a life in relationship with others.

Father's efforts to get Henry the prosthetics he needed eventually took him to another city and state. But, Henry did not leave the Colón home the way he had arrived. He took something with him he couldn't have gotten anywhere else. His heart was packed with love, his spirit was enriched by kindness, and his mind was full of the knowledge that he was a child of God. Nourished physically and spiritually, Henry left the Colón family a new man, pursuing a new life filled with hope.

The friendship that had begun to blossom between Marie and me continued to grow, and we very much wanted our families to meet. She had met my husband and children on her trips to Florida, and she thought our children and husbands would get along well. So, a year after our first meeting, she invited my family to her home for the Fourth of July.

We pulled into the Colón's driveway on a hot and humid summer evening. It had been a ten-hour trip and we were glad to finally arrive at our destination. This was an unusual outing for my family—we had never gone to visit and stay with a family whom we didn't really know.

Marie's son was in the driveway, unloading the trunk of his car. We climbed out of the van and introduced ourselves. He was a good-looking young man, a college student at the University of Georgia. He told us his parents were expecting us, and he invited us into the house. The Colóns received us warmly. Marie and I hugged, the husbands shook hands, and the Colón children took our children to the game room. It seemed Marie was right. The families were getting along well.

At that time, Marie and Paco had taken in a young girl from Bogotá. I knew a little of Ruth's story and had prepared my children. When Ruth was two years old, a gas oven blew up in the family's impoverished home. Ruth was severely scarred by the explosion. She had no nose, no lips, no ears. Her eyelashes and eyebrows were gone. Most of the hair on her head had been permanently lost.

She was also missing a hand. When the explosion happened, she had been carrying her plastic baby bottle. The intense heat caused the bottle to melt instantaneously, fusing the bottle to her hand. Medically, nothing could be done. Ruth's hand had to be amputated. She lost it shortly after the explosion.

Ruth's life deteriorated from there. Her family couldn't deal with her appearance. They ostracized her and gave her no real love or affection. The struggles of their everyday life were already overwhelming, and Ruth's condition just added more burden and stress. They would leave her alone for long periods of time, neglected physically and emotionally. When her father died, things only got worse. By the time she was nine years old, Ruth was living in the sewers of Bogotá.

Some months after meeting her, I interviewed Ruth for a television segment we produced about her. In the interview she told me:

When my father died and my mother had to go to work, I spent a lot of time on the streets. At first I stayed out a couple of hours at a time, then a couple of days at a time, and soon I went to live on the streets altogether. This was very difficult. You don't know what's going to happen from one moment to the next. At night, you wonder if you will wake up in the morning.

Ruth's life on the streets and in the sewers is not an unusual one in Columbia. Abandoned children have long been a problem. In years past, many rural families migrated to the big cities, hoping to find a better life. This created a population greater than the economy could support. Without money, families found themselves in poor living conditions, lacking the basic amenities and services necessary to sustain a reasonable existence. Slums, ghettoes, and worse became the plight of these migrants, and their lives became complicated by all the social problems common to such housing areas. Abandoned families, especially abandoned children, became commonplace. With no adult influence and no adequate means of survival, the children took to the streets, became acculturated to the lifestyle, and began a downward spiral of existence that they passed on to their own children—if they lived long enough to have them.

In the streets and sewers of the city, street children learn the harsh and cruel rules of the subculture. Prostitution, sexual exploitation, criminal behavior, and drug abuse are all part of the experience. So are beatings, rapes, and shootings.

By twelve years of age, Ruth had seen it all. She knew friends who were raped, others who were beaten up for sport, and some who were shot to death as they lay sleeping in alleys and doorways. She wouldn't talk about her own experiences. They were locked tightly in her heart.

Fortunately for Ruth, she was found by a foundation whose mission is to rescue and rehabilitate the street children. They took her from the streets and placed her in a group home to help meet her diverse needs. The foundation hoped that one day they might be able to assist her in finding a plastic surgeon who would agree to reconstruct her face.

Hoping to find a doctor here, the foundation brought Ruth to the United States on fundraising trips. Through them, they hoped someone would see her and donate their services. One such trip brought Ruth to New Orleans.

Dr. Gustavo Colón, a friend of Maries and Pacos though no relation, heard of Ruth's situation. A well-known plastic surgeon, he welcomed the opportunity to help Ruth. In her he saw a bright young girl with a potentially bright future. And he saw a way to give back to the service of God some of the gifts and talents God had given to him.

However, the reconstructive process would take several surgeries. Ruth would need to remain in New Orleans for a year. And throughout that time, she would need consistent and good care. It was asking a lot for someone to take on. Who would take her in? Marie and Paco received the telephone call. "Of course," said Marie, "she can stay here."

By the time my family and I met Ruth, she had gone through the first of those surgeries. Like everyone else, we found Ruth to be bright, confident, and enthusiastic. She was quick to laugh, quick to joke, and quick to tell you what she thought. Ruth was no wallflower; she was in the midst of it all.

Marie enrolled Ruth in school, involved her in outside activities, and worked diligently with her to improve her English. This was an ongoing struggle. Ruth would use her Spanish at every opportunity. Marie finally prevailed by simply not answering her unless she tried to speak in English.

However, Marie was sensitive to the fact that English was a second language for Ruth. She would give her an instant translation of every reading and homily at Mass, and she would even translate an entire movie for her while it was airing. It would have been hard to find a better environment for Ruth—while she received the discipline she needed, she also received plenty of love. Perhaps for the first time in her life, Ruth was catching a glimpse of what the parent/child relationship was all about.

The surgeries progressed well. Through them, Dr. Colón constructed a new nose for Ruth. He created lips for her. And he made her new ears. Using skin grafts, he worked to smooth out the thick scar tissue that had been her face. It was a long and grueling process, but the results were worth the effort.

Through it all, Ruth was a trooper, but her overall cooperation varied.

For example, she refused to wear the heavy elastic facemask that would help to smooth her face tissue, but she was an excellent patient following surgery and diligently worked at her schoolwork while recuperating. With a laugh, Marie remembers teaching Ruth how to kiss once her new lips were healed. Ruth wasn't much for physical affection. She had definitely decided that Puerto Ricans kiss too much. But she seemed anxious to learn how to make her new lips work. Marie taught her how to pucker and Ruth practiced by giving Marie pecks on the cheek. In more than one way, it was a breakthrough moment for Ruth. Prior to this, she would pull away when someone would try to hug her or show her affection. Obviously, loving embraces and affectionate gestures hadn't been a part of her life experience.

In the year that Ruth was with the Colón family, we saw her two more times. Each time my family was amazed by the progress she was making. The surgeries had done much for her appearance; the love had done even more for her heart. Commenting on the ongoing transformation in Ruth, Dr. Gus Colón said in our interview:

She's been through so much physical and emotional trauma. A lot of people with her injuries would stay very depressed. But she is a girl who is trying to improve herself. She's brought love and enthusiasm to me.

Marie couldn't agree more. She added:

Somebody who has gone through as much as she has gives us hope. She has been brought here to start knowing who God is, and how much He loves her. When you see the blooming of that love in her life, her life doesn't seem so tragic. It is the beauty of the cross.

Like the others before her, Ruth eventually left the Colón home. But, as was the case with them, she did not go away empty-handed. Ruth left with a heart full of love, a spirit full of hope, and a life full of promise.

My family's friendship with the Colón family has only grown over the years. In fact, that good-looking young man in the driveway eventually became our son-in-law, and Marie and I, well, we are now *consuegras*, mothers-in-law to each other's children. It has been a blessing getting to know Marie and Paco, and I am certain that sentiment is echoed in the hearts of all who have stayed at *Casa de Colón*.

Heavenly Father:

Everything I have belongs to You.
You have given me so much,
and I am grateful for these gifts.
Beginning today, make me sensitive to the movement of
Your Spirit.
Use me to bless the lives of those around me,
especially those who are most in need of help.
I ask this through Christ our Lord,
Amen.

Healing hearts.
Changing lives.
Saving souls.

Living His Life Abundantly® International, Inc. seeks to "mend the Christian fabric" of today's culture by proclaiming the healing love of Jesus Christ through all manner of media and communications.

Johnnette Benkovic & Fr. Edmund Sylvia, CSC

Living His Life Abundantly®
International, Inc.

Johnnette & Greg Popcak, MSW, LCSW

LHLA accomplishes this mission by producing media which builds up the Body of Christ and encourages a practical application of the Catholic faith in the world today. LHLA evangelizes through six major outlets:

- Television
- Radio
- Conferences
- Internet
- Print
- Resource Distribution

Visit us at www.lhla.org